CONFERENCE
PROCEEDINGS

T0303312

Making Sense of Transnational Threats

Workshop Reports

Gregory F. Treverton

NATIONAL SECURITY RESEARCH DIVISION

The research described in this report was conducted by the RAND National Security Research Division (NSRD).

ISBN: 0-8330-3725-0

The RAND Corporation is a nonprofit research organization providing objective analysis and effective solutions that address the challenges facing the public and private sectors around the world. RAND's publications do not necessarily reflect the opinions of its research clients and sponsors.

RAND® is a registered trademark.

Published 2005 by the RAND Corporation
1776 Main Street, P.O. Box 2138, Santa Monica, CA 90407-2138
1200 South Hayes Street, Arlington, VA 22202-5050
201 North Craig Street, Suite 202, Pittsburgh, PA 15213-1516
RAND URL: http://www.rand.org/
To order RAND documents or to obtain additional information, contact
Distribution Services: Telephone: (310) 451-7002;
Fax: (310) 451-6915; Email: order@rand.org

Preface

In 2003, Global Futures Partnership (GFP) in the CIA's Directorate of Intelligence (DI) Sherman Kent School for Intelligence Analysis and the RAND Corporation embarked upon a project to reconsider what had come to be called "alternative analysis" in the Intelligence Community. The partners did so in light of the growing importance of transnational issues, especially terrorism, but also organized crime and weapons proliferation, among other issues. The starting assumption was that transnational issues presented a different set of analytic challenges than more traditional intelligence topics targeted primarily on nation states. The project focused particularly on the question of how to effectively integrate alternative analysis into the overall analytic and policymaking process for transnational issues, paying comparatively less attention to evaluating specific tools or developing new ones.

The workshops interpreted here brought together a wide range of specialists – from history and culture to cognitive psychology. The rapporteurs' reports on individual workshop reports are thus well worth reading; they are presented in this document, following a summary of the key findings from the project. A more detailed version of the project's key findings, coupled with the results of further research stimulated by the workshops, is published by the Kent School and RAND as *Making Sense of Transnational Threats* (Kent Center Occasional Paper, Vol. 3, No. 1).

This research was conducted within the Intelligence Policy Center (IPC) of the RAND National Security Research Division (NSRD). NSRD conducts research and analysis for the Office of the Secretary of Defense, the Joint Staff, the Unified Commands, the defense agencies, the Department of the Navy, the U.S. intelligence community, allied foreign governments, and foundations.

For more information on RAND's Intelligence Policy Center, contact the Acting Director, Gregory Treverton. He can be reached by e-mail at Greg_Treverton@rand.org; by phone at 310-393-0411, extension 7122, or by mail at RAND, 1776 Main Street, Santa Monica, CA 90407-2138. More information about RAND is available at www.rand.org.

Contents

Tables

Introduction

The project's emphasis on moving beyond "alternative analysis" as now practiced reflected a judgment – an impressionistic one, but one that was widely shared by other participants in the project – that whether for traditional or transnational issues, alternative analysis now is used only episodically in the analytic process and often on less critical issues (such as long-run prospects for a country) and is often viewed more as a supplemental exercise than as an essential component of the overall analytic process, and thus is not particularly effective in influencing analytic judgments even when a serious effort is made to address a key issue.

GFP and RAND convened a series of unclassified one-day workshops from February to September 2003 to examine how to better integrate alternative analysis into the analytic process. The workshops brought together – on a non-attribution basis – analysts from the CIA's DI and from other agencies focused on transnational issues, along with a distinguished group of more than 30 non-governmental experts. These experts came from a variety of disciplines relevant to thinking about the analytic process – cognitive psychology, psychiatry, group dynamics, information technology, organizational studies, knowledge management, artificial intelligence, diplomatic history, technology studies, strategic studies, and even journalism, along with experts in specific transnational domains such as terrorism and proliferation. The aim of the workshops – which featured both formal presentations and break-out group discussions – was to blend the widely varied perspectives of the participants with the aim of generating new ideas that could ultimately yield more concrete proposals. The intent was not so much to provide a detailed roadmap for transforming alternative analysis for transnational issues, but rather to suggest which broad direction this process ought to head.

The workshops took up the question of how to better integrate alternative analysis into the analytic process from four different viewpoints, and the reports on those four workshops in turn constitute the chapters of this report. First, we probed how "transnational" issues such as terrorism differ, analytically, from "traditional" state-centric issues. What special analytic challenges do transnational issues pose, and how may those challenges vary among particular transnational issues? Our distinguished presenters were L. Paul Bremer, then Chairman and CEO, Marsh Crisis Consulting, former Ambassador for Counterterrorism, and later the head of the Coalition Provision Authority in Iraq; Phil Williams, University of Pittsburgh; Amy Sands, Monterey Institute; John Parachini, RAND Corporation; Ernest May, Charles Warren Professor of American History, Harvard University: Baruch Fischoff, Carnegie Mellon University; Dennis Gormley, Consulting Senior Fellow for Technology and Defense Policy, International Institute for Strategic Studies , and Steven Simon, RAND Corporation.

The second session turned to an examination of the difficulties that transnational issues, such as terrorism, pose at the level of individual analysts and small working groups; mind-sets and other obstacles to puzzle-solving and mystery-framing, from three perspectives; individual cognition; cultural bias; and small-group interactions. Our presenters were Rick Herrmann, Mershon Center, Ohio State University; Georgia Sorenson, Jepson Center of Leadership Studies; Baruch Fischhoff; David Charney, psychiatrist; Rob Johnston, Institute for Defense Analyses; and John Hiles, Naval Postgraduate School.

In the third session, the focus moved to an assessment of how transnational issues fit or do not fit with the processes and organizations through which they are currently analyzed. It aimed to develop proposals for organizational change, not neglecting the dramatic (and thus perhaps infeasible) but focusing on what might be doable. We were provoked by the following presenters: Karl Weick, University of Michigan, author of *Sensemaking in Organizations*; Elaine Kamarck, Kennedy School of Government, Harvard University; Daniel Byman, Georgetown University, staff member of Congressional 9-11 Inquiry; Tom Davenport, Director, Accenture Institute for Strategic Change, author of *Working Knowledge: How Organizations Manage What They Know*; Bruce Berkowitz, RAND Corporation and Hoover Institution; Roger Kubarych, Senior Economic Advisor, HVB Americas, Adjunct Fellow, Council on Foreign Relations; and Maj. General John R. Landry (US Army, Retired), National Intelligence Officer for Conventional Military Issues.

Finally, the focus of the concluding workshop was dealing – and communicating – with intelligence's consumers, who are now much more numerous, including new consumers ranging from law enforcement, to foreigners, to the American public. What special challenges – and opportunities – are there in interactions with consumers over transnational issues? To animate the conversation, we had the benefit of comments by Rand Beers, former National Security Council Official; Robert Jervis, Columbia University; Thomas Schelling, University of Maryland; Michael Schrage, MIT Media Lab; Samuel Gardiner, National Defense University; and David Ensor, CNN. To all these good people, we express our thanks for their provocations while absolving them of any responsibility for shortcomings in the lessons that have been drawn.

Summary

September 11 provided graphic testimony to the need to better "connect the dots" in providing warning of potential terrorist threats to the American homeland, and it also underscored the shift in intelligence's targets from states to non-state or transnational actors. These animating challenges were the focus of a series of four fascinating workshops conducted from February to September 2003 by Global Futures Partnership (GFP) in the CIA Directorate of Intelligence's Sherman Kent School for Intelligence Analysis and the RAND Corporation, a project that brought together a wide range of experts on cognition, culture, terrorism, and intelligence. This conference proceedings document contains the reports of the workshops, which are provocative in their own right. A fuller synthesis of the project's results, titled *Making Sense of Transnational Threats,* was published by the Kent School (Kent Center Occasional Paper, Vol. 3, No. 1).

September 11 was, in the words of foreign affairs columnist Thomas Friedman, a "failure of imagination." Many organizations, public and private, that confront uncertainty have developed processes and tools to try to avert such failures. For the Intelligence Community, one set of such tools has become known as "alternative analysis." If traditional intelligence analysis generates forecasts or explanations based on logical processing of available evidence, alternative analysis seeks to help analysts and policymakers to stretch their thinking and to hedge against the natural tendency of analysts – like all human beings – to search too narrowly for information that would confirm rather than discredit existing hypotheses, or to be unduly influenced by premature consensus within analytic groups close at hand.

In the Intelligence Community, alternative analysis has tended to be organized around discrete questions addressed in specific finished products. Thus, it is used only occasionally and then generally for less critical issues, such as long-run prospects for a country. It is often viewed by analysts as more of a supplemental exercise than an essential component of the overall analytic process; therefore, it is not particularly effective in influencing analytic judgments even when a serious effort is made to address a key issue.

The project's premise was that transnational issues do differ, as do targets of intelligence analysis, from more traditional state-centric issues. These differences are displayed in Table 1. To be sure, the differences are matters of degree. For instance, issues regarding weapons of mass destruction (WMD) mix states and non-states. And state-centric issues can share the defining characteristics of transnational issues – they are unbounded, fast moving, and obscured by overwhelming information. In that sense, the challenge facing analysts in comprehending Al Qaeda is not that much different from the ones confronting analysts in the run-up to the Battle of France or Pearl Harbor.

Table 1
Traditional Targets Versus Transnational Targets

Traditional Targets	Transnational Targets
Focus: states; non-states secondary	Focus: non-states; states as facilitators, willingly or not
Nature of targets: hierarchical	Nature of targets: networked
Context: intelligence and policy share basic "story" about states	Context: much less of a shared story about non-states, less "bounded," more outcomes possible
Information: there is too little information, and so priority goes to secrets	Information: secrets are still important, but there are torrents of information;; fragmented
Reliability: secrets regarded as reliable	Reliability: information unreliable
Pace of events: primary target slow moving, discontinuities rare	Pace of events: targets may move quickly, discontinuities all too possible
Interaction effects: limited	Interaction effects: "your" actions and observations have more effect on target's behavior

Intelligence issues are often divided between puzzles (which could be solved with information that is in principle, but perhaps not in fact, available) and mysteries (which are in the future and contingent, and thus cannot be solved through available information). Beyond these two categories, a third might be defined as "complexities." These are problems that can yield a very wide range of sui generis outcomes that defy even probabilistic predictions because of some combination of the following factors – large numbers of actors, perhaps each of small size; lack of formal or informal rules governing behavior; and the large influence of situational as opposed to internal factors in shaping behavior.

The four workshops explored a number of ways, especially more intuitive ways, to address such problems. One way that seemed especially promising was organizational "sense-making," as developed by the noted organization theorist, Karl Weick. Sense-making is a continuous, iterative, largely informal effort to paint a picture of what is going on that is relevant to an organization's goals and needs. This is accomplished by comparing new events to past patterns, or in the case of anomalies by developing stories to account for those anomalies. Organizations that must be highly reliable, such as aircraft carriers or nuclear power plants, face uncertainties that are akin to the uncertainties that the Intelligence Community faces. They develop what Weick calls "mindfulness" – in particular, a preoccupation with failure, both past and potential, and a "learning culture" in which it is safe and even valued for members of the organization to admit errors and raise doubts.

For intelligence, enhancing mindfulness would be a process, not a product. That process would be:

- **Continual**, not discrete or "one-off" efforts. The objective would be to regularly explore different possible outcomes and debate assumptions, all linked to incoming information on the issue under consideration.

- **Creative** and freewheeling, in place of a more formal alternative analysis process, with a strong emphasis on logical argument to come to clear conclusions. It would consciously mix mental biases – for instance, by using a method for building teams akin to the practice that some Wall Street firms use known as "barbelling," which involves pairing young financial professionals with those over 50 to take advantage of both adventurousness and experience. And it would provide time, because ideas most often "pop out" of slow--moving, largely unconscious, contemplative modes of thought, rather than more conscious, purposeful, and analytic ones.

- **Collaborative**, instead of alternative analysis, such as playing devil's advocate or "what-if" analysis, that can be done individually. Indeed, sensemaking might be "public" – that is, orally reviewing assumptions and alternatives "out loud" as a collaborative effort.

- **Counter-intuitive**, seeking disconfirming evidence, rather than confirming evidence, and featuring regular, even if brief and informal, exercises in which analysts focus on how they could be wrong.

- **Consumer-friendly**, which is an enormous challenge since "alternative" anything implies yet more time demands on the part of consumers of intelligence of information. It requires thinking of new intelligence "products," for instance, Rapi-Sims, increasingly sophisticated spreadsheet-based programs that allow consumers to manipulate variables to generate alternative outcomes.

The key ideas for do-able innovations to enhance mindfulness are summarized in Table 2.

Table 2
Ideas and Implementation

Idea	Implementation and Purpose
Employ "analytic methodologists"	Design and facilitate divergent-thinking exercises and structured dialogues aimed at uncovering alternative views
Introduce public sense-making processes	Structured dialogues to consider all possibilities
Use web-logs as a production vehicle	Common, continuous platform for analysis/sense-making and for alternative processes
Consciously mix biases in teams (e.g., "barbelling")	Increase likelihood of alternative interpretations of evidence
Regularly do after-action reports	Look at failures and successes with an eye to drawing constructive lessons
Develop information technology to store and automatically recover hypotheses and ideas	Aid analysts' memory and creative thinking
Provide Rapi-Sims and other opportunities for experiential learning by intelligence consumers	Brief simulations/games to help consumers comprehend range of uncertainty

Alternative analysis needs to be framed as ongoing organizational processes aimed at sustained mindfulness, rather than as just a set of tools that analysts are encouraged to employ. The alternative analysis processes would have to be made a high priority of senior intelligence managers, reinforced by changes in reward structures, production schedules, and staffing requirements to encourage the continued use of these processes. Above all, they require an organizational culture that values and trains for continuous, collective introspection--often difficult to achieve in high-demand, understaffed environments. Could mindfulness-focused organizational processes really enhance warning of emerging transnational threats? No one can confidently answer that question in the affirmative, but reflecting on past surprises in "complex" situations suggests that even modest improvements in organizational processes could make a significant difference in preparedness. What if the concerns of the Phoenix FBI office about flight training before September 11 had not only been shared broadly within the government but also integrated into a mindfulness-focused inter-agency process featuring collaborative sense-making, web-log type forums, and computer-generated references to extant scenarios for crashing airplanes into prominent targets? Might those concerns have garnered far broader attention than they did?

Workshop I: The Analytic Challenges Posed by Terrorism and Other Transnational Issues

February 12, 2003

Headlines

- Transnational issues are puzzles but ones that always will have missing pieces.

- The "puzzle" metaphor should not lead to the fallacy that U.S. actions do not matter with the threat of terrorism. In a real sense, we "co-create" the threat with our enemies.

- Indeed, a threat such as terrorism can be understood only in light of U.S. vulnerabilities. That understanding requires, however, "net assessment"-- or relative comparisons -- of the sort the United States has never really done, and intelligence has hardly ever attempted.

- In the debate over "intelligence failure" before September 11, what is striking is that we do not yet really understand how 9/11 happened to us – how long the attacks were in planning, what the logistics were, how good the terrorists' intelligence was, and so on.

- Organizations probably cannot change fast enough to produce the "collaborative workplaces" that transnational issues require. So the solution is to work around the "edges" of organizations possibly virtually, in ways that will leave existing organizations in place while bringing their capacities together.

Framing the Task

This is the report of the first of four workshops part of a project jointly run by RAND Corporation and the Global Futures Partnership of the CIA's Sherman Kent Center for Analysis. The task of the project is to find useful frameworks that can help analysts ask themselves, "How could I be wrong?" The group's working hypothesis is that so-called transnational issues, like terrorism, are different, analytically, from more classic state-to-state issues. Yet, transnational issues are important in and of themselves, and, thus, there is no need to exaggerate how they differ from other issues. Thus, the challenge is to develop structured techniques for doing better – to be contrarian, to play the devil's advocate, to engage in "serious play," and to employ computers in the service of stretching viewpoints. The task is not to select a particular technique; rather it is to embed a different perspective, to be systematic in challenging presumptions, and to avoid locking in on particular conclusions.

For this first workshop, the presenters were L. Paul Bremer, then Chairman and CEO, Marsh Crisis Consulting, former Ambassador for Counterterrorism, and later the head of the Coalition Provision Authority in Iraq; Phil Williams, University of Pittsburgh; Amy Sands, Monterey Institute; John Parachini, RAND Corporation; Ernest May, Charles Warren Professor of American History, Harvard University: Baruch Fischoff, Carnegie Mellon University; Dennis Gormley, Consulting Senior Fellow for Technology and Defense Policy, IISS; and Steven Simon, RAND Corporation.

As a basis for discussion, transnational issues seem to differ from traditional issues along several dimensions:

- They tend to move faster than the glacial pace of change in the former Soviet Union.

- Much more information may be relevant, but the information may be of much lower quality than that for traditional issues.

- The issues are less "bounded" than traditional issues; evidence, ideas, and outcomes all may cover a wider range

- Information collection is more difficult because the threat is more diffuse, and the volume of information often conceals what is important.

The challenge was to make the project not just interesting but also *useful* – to analysts and policymakers alike. The purpose of this first workshop was to begin to define transnational issues, identify their salient characteristics, and begin to think about the alternative methods available to tackle them.

A View from Consumers

Terrorism may be unique among issues in that it is so dependent on intelligence; without intelligence, there can be almost no terrorism policy. Yet, the intelligence is very hard to come by. That said, the first piece of the puzzle is that the attacks of 2001 were not hard to predict in general, though their specific timing was very hard to predict. Consider the National Commission on Terrorism.[1] Its general predictions, made well before 2001, were prescient. The litany of predictions from the Commission is damning: There would be attacks on the United States; they would be of Pearl Harbor scale; they might involve biological weapons (for which there were then not enough vaccines); Afghanistan would be a sanctuary; Al Qaeda-like organizations would be the threat; the United States lacked human

---

[1] The Commission, also known as the Bremer Commission after its chair, Ambassador L. Paul Bremer, issued a report in June 2000, *Countering the Changing Threat of International Terrorism,* Washington, D.C.: National Commission on Terrorism, 2000. Available at http://www.fas.org/irp/threat/commission.html (last visited December 10, 2004).

intelligence; internal communications within the FBI were bad; and relations between the FBI and the CIA were worse, especially in sharing databases; the United States had taken a narrow approach to wiretaps; there was too little translation capability; borders were uncontrolled; and so on.

September 11: One Consumer View

The above assessment was that of ten citizens, albeit experienced ones. They made three dozen recommendations. Not one of them was adopted at the time they were made, although almost all have been since September 11. Why? The starting point is, perhaps, the Pearl Harbor analogy; we are confident and optimistic as a people. Democracies, especially ours, are bad at long-term planning. But there was no shortage of strategic warning. The threat had been discussed, if not calibrated, by 1995. So what, in more detail, went wrong?

- We didn't believe the threat. There was the Pearl Harbor cultural blockage. In particular, secular America is bound to understate the impact of religious fervor. Plus, there is the legacy of political correctness, which makes it difficult to talk of "Muslim" anything. Intelligence never made a convincing case to policymakers that Al Qaeda was a serious threat to the United States.

- History is "now" for our adversaries but largely forgotten by us. In the 1980s, Charles Pasqua talked of his fear that France's Muslims sought to create the Islamic Republic of France. And he was serious. Few Americans know about 1919, the end of the caliphate and the carving up of the Middle East including (a very artificial) Iraq. But for our foes it is not history; it is now.

- Imagination was lacking. In particular, we had become used to the "old style" terrorism of the 1960s and 1970s – secular, narrow, and restrained. Perhaps Pan Am 103 was the transition, although we didn't see it that way at the time.

- There was the tendency to concentrate on continuity, and not imagine discontinuity. As one workshop participant put it, "There was too much Darwin (evolution), not enough Velikhovsky (discontinuity)."

Attention Please!

Getting the attention of policymakers is also a challenge. There is too much information to absorb. And too little time to do so. In crises, intelligence may have twenty minutes to prepare a case. The lack of time compounds the problem of making assumptions. To be effective, analysts need to be timely, concise, and relevant. In September 1979, one agent report that the Soviets were moving into Kandahar, Afghanistan. In retrospect, it was a crucial piece of evidence, but at the time it was neglected. Why? The prevailing assumption was that the Soviet Union was still happy with Afghanistan as a buffer, or that the Brezhnev Doctrine of intervention didn't operate outside the Warsaw Pact. Yet, what these presumptions overlooked was that the slide of events in Afghanistan had been distinctly unattractive to Moscow, and Moscow was as threatened then by radical Islam in Iran as Russia is now. Moreover, Moscow might have reckoned from the weak U.S. reaction to its actions in Yemen and Angola that it had a free hand in Afghanistan.

Policymakers may be trapped in a particular state-to-state view, and therefore may find it especially hard to comprehend terrorism. They can't send diplomatic notes to Al Qaeda. The inertia of bureaucracy is, as always, critical, and in some ways the better the bureaucracies, the worse the inertia: At the State Department, the counterterrorism chief's biggest problem did not lie elsewhere; rather, it was the regional bureaus that dominate the Department.

Breaking such organizational cultures is no mean feat. As always, there is the need to keep intelligence short and timely, while at the same time *not* avoiding sounding a warning. Waffling is deadly, because policymakers are also decisionmakers.

What is new is that state and local officials are desperate for information but always disappointed when they get it. It is always too ambiguous. The new Terrorist Threat Integration Center (TTIC) raises more questions than it answers; only time will tell whether it can succeed as the central "connector of the dots." The real challenge is moving information upward from states and localities. And who is to integrate foreign and domestic material? Is a free-standing domestic intelligence operation, on the model of Britain's MI-5, the right approach? And how would it get access to private information?

Surely, it is true that making people pay attention to discontinuities is hard, for those discontinuities are inherently "iffy." It is much easier to focus on immediate threats, a theme that recurred in this workshop. Especially now, policy is focused on threats; any attempt to debunk a threat is not heard. How do we move resources toward threats that have not yet developed? The answer to this question implies, "We need to be thinking about what we are *not* thinking about," which is obviously very difficult. Moreover, the structure *forces* more and more material into the public domain because no administration can risk being caught failing to warn of a threat. The result is a "creeping loss of credibility" to any warning. It would help if government, as the private sector sometimes does, spelled out its assumptions before making any major decisions, and then let intelligence do sensitivity analysis.

Is there anything to be learned from the experience of "old Europe"? On the plus side, it has been dealing with this problem for a long time, and has traditions of dealing across center, "state," and local governments. On the minus side, Europe may be tempted to believe that it's beaten this problem, when in fact it's beaten only the 1970s variant of terrorism. And, outside Britain, senior ministers in Europe don't see intelligence.

How can we wall off time for senior officials to reflect, or even to think? How can we address what we're neglecting? For a decade, Al Qaeda has been the main preoccupation, but what will be next? Those who work on international organized crime now have the time to think, and any red-teaming is to the good.

Parsing Transnational Issues

Given this workshop's focus on the nature of transnational issues, *as an analytic challenge,* how do they differ from more traditional issues? And how does a range of such issues – non-proliferation, international organized crime, and terrorism – differ among themselves?

Non-proliferation

In some ways, the current concern over weapons of mass killing is going "back to the future," for non-proliferation analysts were working on "transnational" issues thirty years ago. But the threat does make intelligence analysis more complex, for it increases the targets, the number of players, and the types of expertise needed to do the analysis. And intelligence is critical at all states – from the weapons themselves, to the capabilities, to the doctrine and intent of key actors, to the vulnerabilities of countries of concern, to the impact on allies or regional partners who might be subject to WMD attacks. The nature of the threat could be expanded or held to a tighter focus – nuclear, chemical, and biological weapons and the missiles to deliver them. The states that could proliferate weapons are few in number, but they are the most likely proliferators, at least at the high (nuclear) end. States or non-state groups can jump-start the weapons-acquisition process, so the problem is looming.

For this issue, as for others, the metaphor of a puzzle seemed apt. But these are not only puzzles with missing pieces, but they are also puzzles that are never completed. Even the questions depend on what the analysts' purpose is in doing the analysis. The information sources are intelligence's "INTs" (HUMINT, SIGINT, IMINT) but are also open sources — the databases that are now proliferating as well. So, too, tools need to fit the culture. In the past, for instance, various intelligence services tracked scientific literature, especially in the Soviet Union. But expertise is necessary to understand the nuances of that literature, which is an instance of another theme – the dissolving of the line between information collection and analysis. Collection seems straightforward, but it is huge in scope.

Analytically, the challenge is daunting. Even the best collection of data will supply only random pieces of the puzzle, the amount of data is overwhelming, there are language barriers, technical expertise is in too-short supply, and institutional cultures impose their own barriers. The challenge is to avoid ethnocentrism: the question is not, as it so often is, how would *we* do it, but rather, how would *they* do it. It was, for instance, easy for American analysts to dismiss the idea that India might want chemical, as well as nuclear, weapons. The challenge is to ask why they might. Asking that question requires creating a team, and the team can't be built in the middle of a crisis. Cooperation has to cut across not just expertise from different realms but also national borders. Indeed, the C3 of this business is "community, coordination, and collaboration."

International Organized Crime

International organized crime is film noir, not traditional cinema. What's new? The list is long – "sovereignty-free actors," the new nomads for whom the loss of state status is also a loss of constraints; changing and diminishing of the state; diffusion of power; malevolent social networks; resurgence of the past, such as warlordism; and global opportunities. All this might be called, for intelligence, the Global Borderless Intelligence Space.

In these circumstances, then, the challenge is to think bottom up, not top down; to think market; to think networks; to think of connected layers and of states as puppets, the hosts for parasites. In passing, it seems that the European terror networks were and remained tightly coupled, and so were easy to roll up. Even Al Qaeda may be, using network analysis, a relatively small number of people. There is the upper world and the underworld – although it is critical to keep in mind that while criminals may conceive of themselves as the underworld, terrorists may not. They may think *we* are the underworld. In that sense, our own language and concepts may get in the way. The Balkans are one example; in some regions, only the illicit markets are the ones that work.

Another example is trafficking in women. Thinking of unlikely partners is imperative. International markets can facilitate collusion with legitimate institutions. States more and more are acquiescent to corruption and manipulation. Cosmetic conformity and tacit deceit have become regular practices in some parts of the globe. But skepticism is warranted about connections between terrorism and international crime. Rather, terrorists may "do it themselves."

It is also imperative to ask the Darwinian questions: What if we succeed? How will our foes adapt? We will determine, in that sense, the threat to us. So, we must think in terms of models and patterns and anomalies.

Richards Heuer and others are skeptical of the "mosaic approach" to intelligence, which seeks to assemble evidence. But there may be something to be said for it. Can we imagine "tipping points" where another piece or two of evidence might shift the balance of an argument? Surely, though, competing hypotheses also are important. It is, for instance, easy to imagine Cuba's post-Castro criminal future on the model of another post-communist state, the Soviet Union, but it may be better conceived through the hypothesis of yet another weak Caribbean state.

Terrorism

Again, the metaphor of a puzzle seemed useful. A range of relationships between states and terrorist groups can be conceived. So, too, can disaggregating the "gang of seven" state sponsors that the U.S. government has identified prove to be fruitful, for they differ in how they make (or don't make) decisions – Iran may be more unitary than the others – and some of them will be "allies" in future U.S. campaigns. The more one looks at the system from which terrorist action emerges, as opposed to mere grievance, the larger the states loom.

Still, the data set is and will be very small. What can we infer from the few cases available? A starting point is to ask why terrorists haven't behaved as we thought they would. They haven't, so far, engaged in biological attacks, despite a welter of advertising by us of our vulnerability. We haven't been at all systematic on this score. What, for instance, are the factors that might determine a group's interest in weapons of mass casualty (WMC)? There is a need to identify new metrics for comparison. One useful tool would be measures of sameness and difference. In assessing Aum Shinrikyo, we focused on means, not outcomes. That perhaps played a role in our un-preparedness for September 11, where the key fact was outcome, not means.

Terrorists do leave "digital footprints" when they communicate, travel, and need money. Tracking those footprints runs into traditional constraints borne of privacy and security. Moreover, the process is reactive: we might act, and they would react. But, still, if Wal-Mart can update its inventory every evening, and send the results to its suppliers, doing better at tracking footprints shouldn't be beyond our wits.

In discussing these issues, the balance between warning and inviting unwelcome action was key: how and how much do we inform localities, not to mention citizens, without advertising our vulnerabilities. The biological threat is a perfect example. Red-teaming was frequent and familiar during the Cold War; now, it is harder to do but more important. Catch words suggest why this is so: information "corridors" and the fact that law enforcement is caught in its own "horizontal stovepipes" – i.e., cases. There needs to be a conceptual framework for examining these issues that must include a willingness to be open to new concepts and structures. Analysis of the problem of terrorism must be adaptive if it is to keep pace with the evolving nature of the threat.

Two final concerns emerged. The metaphor of a puzzle is powerful and apt. Yet, especially as distinguished from "mysteries," it tends to imply that (a) there is a solution if only we could find it; and (b) that solution is mostly independent of U.S. action. To be sure, terrorist groups are obscure, so the puzzle has many pieces. Moreover, not only is the range of "U.S." actions – from diplomacy, to war, to finance, to black operations – that might shape those groups broad, skepticism about how much they can be shaped is warranted. Still, to regard those groups as being entirely exogenous from U.S. actions would be a serious mistake.

Similarly, transnational threats do seem, on a first approximation, very different from traditional threats. Yet, we seem to use the same models to attempt to understand them. Is that an error? Finally, we need to think of what "just in time" would mean for intelligence analysis.

Learning from Classic Intelligence Failures and September 11

The following three classic examples of intelligence failure have both elements in common with and lessons that apply to September 11[t] and beyond.

Operation Barbarossa

We now know Stalin ignored more than a hundred signals of the German invasion. Why? As in other cases, the first reason was the *system*. In the Soviet system, there was but one intelligence consumer, Stalin. He compartmented and coveted information. To say that his actions discouraged disagreement is an understatement, for his favorite line about a disagreeable estimate was, "I have no further use for this work."

Yet, Stalin was also powerfully the prisoner of his preconceptions. He believed that Hitler had learned from World War I not to start a two-front war. And he also knew that Britain was trying its best to bring Moscow into the war, and so he discounted everything that came to Moscow through British intelligence.

Pearl Harbor

Here, too, there were signals aplenty, from MAGIC to radio intercepts, and the system played a powerful role. The Army and Navy divided the decryption task, rather than cooperating, so neither saw the total picture. There was no comparison of the intelligence take and no analysis of it. The shear volume of information helped to ensure that key pieces of information were lost in the surrounding "noise."

Consumer habits were also powerful. Even in 1941, consumers were busy and distracted. Herbert Feis, then an advisor to the Secretary of State, recalled how he stopped reading the intercepts for fear he would reveal something secret inadvertently. U.S. preconceptions were a critical aspect of this intelligence failure. The cultural presumptions about Japan were as strong then as ours were about the Arab world in 2001: they made only cheap toys. Moreover, they surely wouldn't attack because they understood the U.S. Congress well enough to know that would bring America into the war. Breaking through all these presumptions would have required someone who was both an expert on Japan (like U.S. Ambassador Grew) *and* who had the trust of President Roosevelt (like Harry Hopkins).

France 1940

The French Army's Second Bureau (Deuxieme Bureau) was a very powerful centralized service. Not only had it doubled all the German agents in France, it could tap domestic phones. It had ENIGMA from the Poles, and so was able to read all German Air Force communication. In this case, the intelligence obstacle was mostly systemic. This marvelous intelligence agency was low status even in the French Army. Its customers wanted only raw data, not analysis (*plus ça change?*). For instance, a plotting of its observations of German reconnaissance planes, in the air after a long absence, would have identified the German invasion route *almost precisely*.

The French did understand the Blitzkrieg, or Germany's operational methods, because they had seen them in Poland, and they did not hold to any "Maginot myth" (the line held in its sector). But they did assume that Germany's armored spearheads required level terrain, which reinforced the view that the attack would come, as it had in World War I, through Belgium. That was the German starting point as well.

How does any of this apply to September 11? It will be a long time before history decides between the competing hypotheses about surprise. Was it an intelligence success (as George Tenet argues) because we understood the problem, but tactical warning was impossible; or an intelligence failure (Richard Shelby) because we failed to anticipate? Between these A and F grades, history probably will award something between a B and a D.

The lessons may be sharpest from that unhappy success, Germany attacking France. The Germans understood their own weakness, and they, too, had planned on an attack through Belgium. The Ardennes plan arose only because Hitler demanded an attack, and once the high commanders decided they couldn't kill or remove him, they seriously debated what to do. What arose was an unusual collaboration between intelligence and policy. Unlike in France, hard thinking about the enemy came to be prized in Germany. Also unlike France, intelligence officials in Germany had rotated through field and command assignments. They came to be trusted, and to play in war games, as deep experts on France. Hard thinking about the enemy ensued. Through the fusion of military planning, intelligence, and a deep cultural understanding of the enemy, a strategy evolved. The games showed that the Belgian attack was a clear loser. None of the Germans fancied that the Ardennes plan could be a success – the commander, Halder, ranked it one in ten – but it was better than sure failure.

The Classic Intelligence Failures and Transnational Issues

September 11 displayed its own systemic features, miscommunications, and assumptions about what could and couldn't happen. The case of 1940 France suggests a number of lessons. We still don't really understand what happened to us on 9/11. When was it planned? How good were the logistics and the intelligence? We can't know how well or badly we did until we know more about the other side. That should lead to more red-teaming, to more getting in the shoes, if not the heads of Al Qaeda. It also suggests that intelligence needs to get, somehow, the validation of operations. Although very much harder, it also suggests the need for *net assessment*; Germans could judge France in 1940 only against their own plans, and we can really understand the terrorist threat only in light of our own vulnerabilities. The Pentagon has long had an office called "net assessment," and it has done interesting, unconventional analysis. But it has never really become a focal point for understanding the net of *their* threat and *our* capabilities. Nor, for all the red-teaming, has anywhere else in the government done better. Surely, intelligence hasn't.

Finally, if a puzzle is the analogy, the right puzzle is probably not of the jigsaw type but British crosswords, where greater imagination is needed and the clues are few and elusive. The very term puzzle implies that a right answer exists and that that the threat is independent, when actually we can affect the nature of the threat or, to continue the analogy, the design of the puzzle.

Shaping the Project

The next sessions of the project deal, in sequence, with cognitive and analytic obstacles, organizational issues, and questions about communicating with and helping consumers.

Cognitive and Analytic Issues

Behavioral research may be useful because all people face the same multiple problems. In cognitive psychology, the diagnosis and the prescription have drifted apart over time. At the level of communicating with the public – a key subject of the project – doing badly can not only create a sense of helplessness but also undermine the public's faith in authorities (and vice versa).

In thinking about the cognitive challenges of analyzing transnational issues, we conclude the following:

- Biases are a problem. What we do well is also a problem.

- Self-awareness or reflection is difficult, at the time or even in hindsight. What we need is some external calibration.

- Humans can't change their way of thinking very fast without losing control. So measured transitions are key.

- Missing pieces pose the greatest threat and are the most common cause of failure mode. This argues for an integrated assessment.

- Modeling the system is hard, especially when including analysts because of self-serving biases or lack of self-awareness.

- Complexity requires a mental model – a script or schema – for information processing.

- Humans overestimate common knowledge, along with their ability to communicate. What is required is a platform for an integrated assessment; the team investigating the anthrax letters that were mailed after 9/11 eventually became just that. Such a platform needs to link analysis and communication, and analysts and consumers.

- The final lesson was that we "co-evolve" with our enemies, a point that had been made earlier. How can we educate the American people and ourselves without displaying our vulnerability to our enemies?

Organizational Issues

During the Cold War, red-teaming was much more frequent. In one exercise, a laboratory spent years red-teaming Soviet engineering. There was considerable continuity among the participants, which was good but also made for stakeholders with considerable inertia. In the case of one Soviet facility, there was intense concentration on the facility itself, and analysts developed mental stakes in their views of that facility. It proved to be difficult, but necessary, to look beyond the facility to the broader system, and, in particular, to broaden the issue to ask what was going into and emerging from that facility as well.

Structured techniques are imperative for analyzing such messy issues. One such tool is being developed for NRO to explore the behavior of hard targets. In developing GENOA I and II, DARPA focused first on crisis management for the national security agencies. It suggested there was need to look beyond existing intelligence organizations for other models – for instance, less hierarchical ones. Fritz Ermarth, a wise intelligence veteran, asked a decade ago why intelligence was still, at the end of the twentieth century, organized hierarchically, like the Roman legions. These examinations face the problem of how to overcome cognitive bias.

Probably, the right approach is to operate at the "edge" of organizations, rather than trying to destroy old organizations or create new ones. If those "edges" could come together in collaborative workspaces, probably virtual ones, they would be the ideal. The process would raise not only issues of technical security, but also questions about whether the collaboration needed, or did not need, to be synchronous in time. However, the default approach will be to integrate intelligence in one physical workspace, and that will be all the more likely because there is no constituency for collaborative workplaces.

Transnational issues also call for much more integration of intelligence and policy, and for integrating intelligence and policy outside of the crisis context. Operating in this shifted context may create an opportunity for policymakers to limit ambiguity and therefore better respond to it. How to make this context a reality? September 11 was our "Pearl Harbor," but as a response, the TTIC seems pretty pale. The intelligence community is developing a system for sharing secret compartmented information (SCI) material, and it would be instructive to ask DARPA to report on its experiments.

In an important sense, intelligence can't win. If intelligence is on the mark, it's often ignored, as it was in Somalia in 1993 as the mission of the U.S. and UN forces changed. In that case, the failing was almost ideological, and the intelligence assessment was devalued and ignored when it ran counter to the Clinton Administration's policy agenda. In other cases, like the attack on the USS Cole, the culprit is institutional interest. The State Department wanted a visible presence in Yemen as part of its efforts to maintain good relations, despite intelligence that indicated that presence was imprudent, and there was no operational reason for the Cole to be there.

Do intelligence and policy need to get closer together? It is arguable that they are close already, and sometimes getting closer can be bad. In the 1990s, intelligence did impressive analysis on stability issues in the Middle East, analysis that was linked to an innovative collection program. But that work had little or no effect. In the middle of a virtual U.S. war in Iraq, there was the mind-set that political Islam was a spent force, and so the analysis was ignored. Worse, as a result of this consumer disinterest, the CIA "stopped listening to itself."

How do you assure allocation of resources to issues that are peripheral and not currently a focus of policymakers?

Earlier, this discussion implied that policy shouldn't question the presumptions of analysts – for instance, presumptions about threats. But why not? In 1998, the NSC held meetings to examine threats, and intelligence found those meetings intrusive; intelligence didn't want others questioning its assumptions. Policy does try to stick intelligence with judgments that force action; this is particularly the case for one category of policymakers, those in Congress, when they do not entirely trust the Executive Branch. They are tempted to turn policy questions into intelligence ones, by saying that a certain intelligence finding will trigger a policy action. But sometimes the Executive tries to stick intelligence with policy judgments as well, as occurred with the targeting decisions made in 1998 after the embassy bombings in Africa, or still later in targeting Osama bin Laden when the Bush administration simply didn't want to take responsibility for the targeting decisions.

Breakout Groups

Breakout groups in the workshops were charged with, in effect, designing a draft agenda for the workshops on each of the three topics -- cognitive and analytic obstacles, organizational issues, and communicating with and helping consumers. The groups were asked to not produce answers at this stage, only good questions, along with ideas about what kind of expertise or papers might be useful in setting up the workshops. Here are their reports:

Analytic and Cognitive Issues

What does "alternative analysis" mean? Are transnational issues harder or different from more traditional issues? Do we risk simply assuming that they are harder? In revisiting these issues, it was noted that we lack a baseline from which to approach any issue. If we assume or suspect that transnational issues are especially tricky analytically, then it will be especially important for the analytic community to be explicit in its assumptions and the logic of its arguments. Frameworks for sifting through evidence need to be clear.

In addition, this group explored the contrast between harder and softer information, because transnational issues may have more of the latter. In other words, it is hard to discern the intentions and capabilities of transnational actors. Another issue is the traps that may be inherent in particular models. A third is the difficulties that arise because the *number* of observations, data points, or cases may be very limited now, although those numbers perhaps are growing. Thus, it is necessary to begin building databases, to establish baselines for threats, and to find ways to cross-validate pieces of evidence. It will also be useful to "suspend" information that is not visibly useful now but may be in the future.

Transnational issues impose the need to work fast and under stress, which probably does not distinguish them from more classic issues. The need to "suspend ambiguity" may be new, and the necessity to work in teams is obvious, but it clashes with the generally introverted personalities of intelligence analysts. The FBI has begun to build "bulletin boards" as a basis for conversation, with information that does not emerge entirely from cases. Ultimately, how can the system be structured to permit, and even encourage, people to think?

Organizational Issues

How can uncertainty be shared? How, in particular, how can we deal with outliers? New tools are needed, but time management may be the key; the firm SRI is doing work on that score for DARPA. There is, again, a premium on reshaping organizations, including virtual ones, rapidly, because issues will arise for which there is no "center." It might be worth looking at other models for collaboration – NASA and weather forecasting in the public sector, or LL Bean and its "mistake of the month" in the private sector. What kind of incentive structures can be developed to for enhancing information sharing?

One particular issue will be the generational differences in the intelligence world. Now, Gen X'ers and Gen Y'ers are being managed by baby boomers. How can intelligence get and keep the best young talent? In terms of possible studies, one outlining the state of the art in tools and techniques for alternative analysis, with private-sector as well as public-sector experience , would be helpful. So, too, might something on the time crunch.

Connecting to Consumers

In an important sense, transnational issues raise basic questions: What is intelligence, and what is policy? As policy and policymakers become more diffuse, connecting to policy becomes harder for intelligence, which understandably prefers predictable processes. The very nature of the consumer appears to be evolving. Now, not only federal policymakers, but also state and local leaders as well as the media and the public, are consumers. All of these consumers need more information faster. By the same token, as the threat of terrorism changes, phone records or other items, some of which are not secret, if not always easily available, might become key intelligence. The FBI is tracking anomalous financial deals as possible parts of financing for terrorists. If rapid sharing of intelligence is imperative, leaks will become inevitable.

In discussing the temptation for policymakers to turn policy questions into intelligence ones, the distinction between offense and defense arose. Intelligence may have an easier time when the United States is on the offensive, for it at least bounds the problem, and the probes that offense entails may produce evidence by stressing the networks of adversaries. By contrast, when the United States is on the defensive, threats may arise from almost anywhere. Over-warning seems almost inevitable; even if it is only a public relations exercise, there can be some costs with warning in terms of having to reveal something of intelligence's sources and methods. . British or Israeli experiences in dealing with their publics might be informative.

On the positive side, games that let policymakers "fly through" scenarios are becoming better and better, but getting policymakers to take the time to use them is always a challenge. On the negative, "demonizing" our adversaries, however understandable it may be, not only is a bar to understanding them; it occurs while we seem to be losing the wider global battle for hearts and minds. In any event, we do "co-create" the threat with those adversaries. So, not only is it critical to take religion into account, doing net assessment would also be ideal.

Workshop II: Dealing with Analytic Biases Borne of Cognition, Culture, and Small-Group Processes

April 2, 2003

Headlines

- For all the talk about the "clash of cultures," it is striking that some of the closest U.S. allies in the Middle East and Persian Gulf are the states most different from us culturally. And our bitterest foes are the most secular, least-Islamic of the states.

- Cop versus spy versus soldier yields at least three distinct types of intelligence – investigative or operational, strategic, and tactical. Interestingly, transnational issues– organized crime, narcotics, terrorism, and weapon proliferation – cross over all three types.

- Research across intelligence's analytic organizations found that most of them are risk averse, generally not fertile grounds for new methods, and prone to do most training on the job – a critique that sparked contention in the group.

- Computer-enabled "thinking tools" offer great promise in enhancing analysts' range of analysis by blending deductive and inductive modes of thought and processing huge amounts of data. Yet, it is important to remember that the "map is not the terrain," and models are models, not reality.

Framing the Task

This is the report of the second of four workshops part of a project jointly run by the RAND Corporation and the Global Futures Partnership of the CIA's Sherman Kent Center for Analysis. The task of the project is to find useful frameworks to help analysts ask themselves, "How could I be wrong?" The group's working hypothesis is that so-called transnational issues, like terrorism, are different, analytically, from more classic state-to-state issues. Yet, transnational issues are important in and of themselves, and, thus, there is no need to exaggerate how they differ from other issues. The first workshop focused on the issues themselves, asking how – along dimensions relevant to analysis – they differed from more traditional issues and how the varied among themselves.

In this second workshop, the focus was on the individual analyst. What, from his or her perspective, are the obstacles to better analysis that are imposed by features of human cognition, by cultural biases, or by the effects of small-group processes? Do those obstacles differ in interesting ways from obstacles to analysis of more traditional issues? And what ideas, techniques, or measures might help in improving the analysis of these issues? For this workshop, our outside presenters were Rick Herrmann, Mershon Center, Ohio State University; Georgia Sorenson, Jepson Center of Leadership Studies; Baruch Fischhoff; David Charney, Psychiatrist; Rob Johnston, Institute for Defense Analyses; and John Hiles, Naval Postgraduate School.

Cognition, Culture, and Small-Group Processes

Thinking About Cognition

Because they often take place at a subconscious level, it is worth being explicit and systematic about cognitive issues. To make sense of uncertainty, people naturally use their own tried-and-true heuristics for filtering data. When it comes to analyzing complex problems, what has worked before will probably work again. The problem is that individuals often rely on these frameworks without ever updating them when they can no longer explain new data. This lack of updating can produce somewhat predictable biases. Put another way, relying on what worked in the past can sometimes spell trouble for objective analysis of problems we deal with today. For instance, we tend to find clues to the probability of an event happening in the future in how easy it is to remember a similar event in the past. But that tendency courts danger when appearances are deceiving, when memory retrieval is primed by emotion or something apart from the event, and when the past isn't a good predictor of the future.

One factor complicating cognitive awareness is that self-reflection is hard, both at the time of an event and in hindsight. We can't change our ways of thinking too fast without losing cognitive control, which can allow uncertainty to overwhelm us. In these situations, people also tend to overestimate both common knowledge and their own communication skills. Moreover, an inability to communicate clearly is one of the reasons why awkward views are expressed and then censored by those that do not understand or cannot understand them.

Overall performance can be improved by using multiple approaches – for instance, modelers, domain specialists, and cognitive experts – because: (a) People can learn from one another's perspectives; (b) the biases can cancel one another. For that learning to occur, a group (organization, society) needs non-exclusionary discourse, while lending an ear to different modes of analysis and expression. For that to happen, must be:

(a) A coherent critique of each approach, so as to get the most out of it and to restrain the claims made in its behalf.

(b) Self-insight and self-discipline, regarding one's cognition, emotions, and social behavior.

(c) A social structure that recruits, nurtures, and retains the right mix of people; leadership that shields analytical work from larger influences Mixing internal and external expertise is crucial. The internal expertise may be captured by the organization's conventional wisdom, but at least the holders of that expertise will have that wisdom.

- There are several classes of analytic procedures, and an audit could be performed on any one of them: Scenarios

- Intuition

- Gaming and role playing

- Playing the devil's advocate

- Rational actor

- Perceptual pattern recognition

- Statistical pattern extraction

- Simulation and modeling.

In the end, an integrated assessment is needed that would focus on risk, but would do so by exploiting the research on sensitivity: What is it that we don't know much about? That audit of an internal assessment can allow the researcher to give equal space to various forms of expertise while allowing the researcher to stay in the cognitive comfort zone; it can accommodate incremental improvements. Representing the assessment graphically can facilitate further review, encourage patience while also producing continuing discomfort over gaps in the assessment, and make it easier to analyze systemic effects – for instance, for the risk of anthrax or smallpox attacks.

Myths About Culture

As the "Headline" above states, for all the talk about the "clash of cultures," some of the closest U.S. allies in the Middle East and Persian Gulf, like Saudi Arabia, are the states that are most different from us culturally. And our bitterest foes, like Iraq, are the most secular, least-Islamic of the states. Cultural differences are, thus, part of the conflict but by no means the whole story. If states are prepared to cooperate with us, cultural differences become less important. If they aren't so prepared, then we tend to attribute the problem to "cultural differences."

Values do differ, but they do not seem to be highly correlated with conflict. What does matter is not sheer cultural differences but rather whether another culture is deemed inferior to our own. The three key judgments in this area concern the interdependence of goals – can we cooperate or not?; relative power; and cultural stakes.

Against this backdrop, propaganda or stereotyping of cultures is not purely rationalization. It is more valid than that. If someone you like is criticized, it is difficult to hear that criticism.

That leads to what psychologist call "balance" or "motivated bias." If the person criticized is close to you – a family member, for instance – it is nearly impossible to change your view of the person. So, instead, you dismiss the information. This tendency results in several all-too common stereotypes or negative images:

Enemy. In this image, the foe is evil, offensive, and clever but often also a paper tiger that will collapse if we stand firm. This image makes it easier to fight, even kill, the enemy, or even to commit "atomic elimination." This image may conflate the regime and people, e.g., "They're all Nazis." At the same time, this image does not necessarily presume that the enemy is a cultural inferior, quite the contrary. In the case of both Germany and the Soviet Union, there was no presumption that their cultures were inferior; indeed, we sometimes worried that they might be superior – in science, math, literature, or dance.

Imperial power. This image and the next (Colony) are two sides of the same asymmetric coin. In this image, a very powerful other state is driven by economic advantage. That other state exercises power indirectly; its empire is "informal." Local agents are its hidden hand, mounting devious conspiracies at every turn. That image breeds such a feeling of powerlessness in the face of the imperial foe that it all but prohibits learning. Everything that happens is other-determined. This image, too, permits killing and may drive imperial-power nations toward autarky.

Colony. This image sees other countries as being divided between the good citizens and the bad ones, with hardly any in the middle. "Good" means they are prepared to cooperate with us, while the "bad" are xenophobic, seek to return their country to the 12th century, and hate us. Earlier, and sometimes now, the bad guys are seen as being supported by an enemy power (before, it was the Soviet Union). At the same time, however, the good guys are not up to acting on their own; they need us in a kind of paternal way.

This image tends to deny indigenous nationalism and to assume the primacy of economics. It, thus, would make it difficult for someone to comprehend a Gamal Nasser. It underscores, too, how much difference it makes whether another country is regarded as a colony or an enemy – the distinction turning on whether that other country is regarded as a cultural equal or an inferior. Under this distinction, people can do things to those they regard as inferior that they would never do to those who they regard as culturally equal. The Nazis occupied both France and Poland but regarded the two very differently. France was seen as a cultural equal, and thus it was to be restored, and its cultural icons were respected. Poland, by contrast, was seen as a cultural inferior, and its museums, theaters, and other icons were destroyed.

What can be done? We first need to understand the stereotypes and how deep they may run, including those in our own work. Part of this understanding is recognizing patterns of misperception. Scenario analysis is also helpful. So many times we have presumed that Tito, or Castro, or Kim Jong Il will collapse long before did or ever will. Scenarios can help us to resist that temptation. That said, though, the risk with scenarios is that in fleshing out a very dubious premise into a full-blown scenario that dubious premise is made more believable. Tom Clancy's novels do that regularly.

Then, perhaps, the right course is to develop a second full-blown scenario to challenge the first, in order to open our minds. If so, then it is important to be fastidious about likelihoods, and not let the probability of several scenarios total to well over 1.0. In accomplishing that task, computers and other aids can help to keep us honest.

Do other cultures recognize that they are stereotyping us? On the whole, the answer is "yes." To be sure, it hardly works to confront them directly with "their" stereotype; it is better to talk about the United States and let them form their own opinions. In general, people find it much easier to recognize others' stereotypes than the ones that imprison themselves. In many instances, it is relatively easy to predict how a country or group will "spin" a view of events and, therefore, it is not hard to predict future propaganda. Should it really be that hard, then, to see how that propaganda will be perceived in other countries? Most people's fantasies are self-serving. The change in Chinese students in the United States over a generation is striking, but it is hard to know how much that represents change in China or simply the students learning what Americans are really like.

Auditing Group Processes

Analysis is almost always done in small groups, so attention to the effects of those groups on analysis is critical. Groups are systems, and systems are mirrors. Those two points are critically important.

Groups have to be seen as systems. They cannot be appreciated from the perspective of an individual, because it is possible for group members to disagree, even sharply, yet still sustain a cohesive group. Individual behavior in groups is not pre-destined, but people do have their individual tendencies. Some, for instance, because of their personalities, will be inclined toward being peacekeepers in the group. The group, however, will need different leadership at different times.

Groups that are systems are also mirrors, or, as Buddhists say, "as above, so below." Problems within the group will be mirrored in its projects, and vice versa. That means that interventions can take place at either level. Suppose a member is habitually late. That may be simply a personality trait, but it also may represent reluctance to participate when faced with the work at hand. In any case, it is important to know what is going on with the group.

There is also the data close to home. In organizations as different as Enron, the FBI, and the shuttle program, there were people fretting but not being heard, and people staying home sick – another early warning sign that was not heard. There is no substitute for looking at what is going on around us.

In an audit of the White House, the person interviewing National Security Council members started taking notes on the attention those members paid to secrets and began to see laxness, given their cavalier attitude toward secrecy. It took a small crisis – the loss of critical secret notes – to prompt the team to come together and realign itself. In another case, a senior female faculty member was having an affair with a younger male colleague, unbeknownst to the rest of the faculty. But the other faculty members began seeing other such older-younger couples everywhere. The knowledge of the affair had spilled out in a pre-conscious way. Freudian slips can be good tip-offs; Washington, D.C., Mayor Marion Berry, who had reported drug problems, slipped on one occasion and described his proposal for drug-free zones around schools as "education-free drug zones."

These observations suggest that purely virtual groups will be subject to danger. If the membership is stable, group-think may result. If it is not, there may be not enough trust. So, some face-to-face interaction is important. RAND, which has to be a highly virtual organization given its offices in several regions of the United States and countries overseas, is a good illustration; mistrust, even feuding, can go one for months between colleagues who don't know one another and feel that they are too busy to make a phone call, let alone make a visit.

Building trust in horizontal organizations means developing a tolerance for errors. What about overcoming the divide between scientists and humanists, in any of its thousands of manifestations? Graphics can help provide a common reference point. For the non-quantitative individuals in an organization, the graphics will be "gosinta" diagrams – this "goes into" that – while for the quantitative individuals in the organization, the graphics will be an invitation to crunch numbers. Sports teams may suggest the utility of laying out roles and being explicit about the cultural rules: We will behave "as if" the rules were thus and such.

Break-Out Groups, I

The three break-out groups were challenged to work from one of the three perspectives but not to be strait-jacketed by them. The first reports from the groups were brief:

Cognition

Transnational issues present cognitive challenges, which could be described as multiple interconnected puzzles. These challenges require methodologies to provide a structured approach for arranging the pieces of the puzzles. While there are multiple ways of examining these problems, there is no one right way because any approach has both truths and biases. Bias can skew the analytic process in different ways. Bias that is inherent is accepted bias, which tends to suppress other biases. Competing bias can result in a synergy or fusion of biases. In response, steps need to be taken to ameliorate some of the danger of becoming stuck in patterned thinking; these steps may include non-exclusionary discourse, articulated critique, and disciplined self-insight.

Culture

How does Osama bin Laden differ from the Serbian gangs? Or does he? The temptation to stereotype is inevitable. First, information is in short supply, and the shorter the supply of information, the greater the temptation to stereotype. The less we know of one another, the more we will impute behavior to intrinsic traits. By contrast, we have lots of context on ourselves and so impute our behavior much less to intrinsic traits. Moreover, with terrorists, our emotions are engaged. And the targets of our analyses are doing stereotyping of their own.

Transnational issues seem to require giving equal weight to evidence of all sorts, but the CIA culture emphasizes secrets. Even language imprisons us. Drug traffickers may think of themselves as being engaged in "criminal" activity, but terrorists surely don't – yet, we lump them together as criminals.

Even if cultural differences are often overstated, culture still matters. We often make mistakes by focusing on the most "Westernized" of foreigners. Most Iranians really *do* have an imperial image of the United States. If those states and their leaders are not "crazy," culture does affect their strategic choices. Even if we could comprehend suicide bombing – or recognize that some of what passes for heroism in our society is nearly suicidal – suicide bombing is not in our strategic repertory. Yet, even in that sense, power matters. We were quite prepared to kill enemy civilians in war a half century ago. Now, we don't have to, or at least not very much.

Small-Group Processes

Small groups are often characterized by intolerance for error, and so the trick is to find ways to challenge conventional wisdom and to provide room for creativity. In that sense, diversity within small groups is critical, and that diversity should range across professional backgrounds, ethnicity, and outlooks. We have long known from social science research that, in general, specialists are the *least* likely to imagine discontinuities, for they know all too well the factors that determine, and perhaps over-determine, the present. It will take outsiders coming at an issue afresh to ask "why not?" That questioning, then, might induce the specialists let their intuition carry them beyond the empirical data at hand.

Because being an outlier in a group is uncomfortable, sustaining diversity in a group is important. There will be too many temptations to arrive at consensus in pursuit of collegiality. Leaders play a critical role in sustaining diversity of opinions. That leadership is different from "management" or "authority." The authority figure in a group may not be the group's real leader.

From the Minds of Spies to Other Minds

Perhaps the process of moving into a new psychological territory, the mind of the spy, can provide some lessons for moving into the new terrain of terrorism and for dealing with other transnational issues.

- Louis Pasteur said, "Chance favors the prepared mind." A new "piece" of evidence can come from anywhere; the challenge is to be open to it. Other disciplines may react negatively to new thinking. But, as stated earlier, "the map is not the territory," and while it is important to know who is in charge of the "map," it is also important not to criticize those who are open to new thinking.

- Familiarization trips are key to understanding the mind of a terrorist. Visit terrorists. It is now possible. The visit can't be hit and run, but people do want to confide. Therefore, it is possible, with time, to create a bubble of intimacy that will enable you to hear terrorists' life stories as they want to tell them. Full immersion is key.

- The familiar intelligence challenges apply. All intelligence tends to be fuzzy and ambiguous, and the challenge is to sort signal from noise, patterns from ground effects. As the Chinese put it: To be uncertain is to be uncomfortable. To be certain is to be ridiculous.

- Head and gut interact. Verbal sparring with trusted colleagues can be fruitful because we often don't know what we know until we say it aloud. But it can't be said to oneself; it has to be said to another who also has knowledge of the subject.

- Many decisions made under intense pressure are right in medicine, war, or intelligence. The reason is that, again, the decision may be based on some very subtle difference that we were not aware of until the decision had to be made. For example, a U.S. ship commander made the correct decision regarding a missile target, perhaps because the radar signature of the threatening *Silkworm* Chinese missile was subtly different from that of a friendly F-4, even though the commander wouldn't have been able to say beforehand how it was so or even that it was so.

The Impact of Analytic Cultures

The culture of organizations plainly matters to the style of analysis. For one researcher, interviews with virtually all the intelligence agencies, plus participating in teams and observing training, yielded intriguing and provocative provisional findings:

If the workshop's subject is "alternative analysis," then the question is, *alternative to what?*, because there seems to be no baseline for a standard analytic method. Instead, the tendency is to rely on previous products of analysis, with some group brainstorming – thus, producing a bias toward confirming earlier views. The validating of data is questionable, and there seems a tendency to look for data that confirms, not refutes, prevailing hypotheses. For instance, "cleaning" of spy reports by the Directorate of Operation (DO) doesn't permit testing of the reports' validity.

The process is risk averse, with considerable managerial conservatism. There is an overemphasis on accuracy, and much less emphasis on surprise. Neither, perhaps, is surprising since young analysts, especially, fear being wrong, and older intelligence analysts face policymakers who don't want surprise; they are able just to cope, so surprises are very unwelcome. Daily written products, especially the President's Daily Brief (PDB), drive the analytic process, and the PDB could be caricatured as "CNN + Secrets" (with its a short-event horizon).

Different agencies have different agendas, procedures, technologies, and meaning – cop versus spy versus soldier, yielding at least three distinct types of intelligence: investigative or operational, strategic, and tactical. Interestingly, transnational issues – organized crime, narcotics, terrorism, and weapon proliferation – run across the three types. Some of the more peripheral analytic elements are more interesting. The Drug Enforcement Administration (DEA) performs all three types of intelligence. It created a tactical intelligence arm distinct from the military's Special Operations Command (SOCOM), and it does investigative intelligence because its relations with the FBI are so frayed. The Counterterrorism Center (CTC) also performs several kinds of intelligence.

Across the analytic agencies studied for this project, the same traits recurred. One was that none of the agencies had much familiarity with the analytic techniques of the others. Among all, there tended to be an overemphasis on writing/communication skills and much less emphasis on analytic methods. Training was driven more by individual analysts than by any strategic view of the agency and its needs. Most training was done on –the job.

The research suggests the need for serious study of analytic methods and for professional methodologists. There should be much more fieldwork for analysts. A central repository of analytic lessons learned would make sense, as would after-action reviews and more formal reviews of strategic intelligence products; those reviews should go to lessons for both individuals and teams, and should look at the root of errors and failures. Oral and written histories would serve as other sources of bases for lessons.

The analytic agencies should aim to create "communities of practice," with mentoring, analytic practice groups, and various kinds of on-line resources, including forums on methods and problem solving. These communities would be linked to the repository of lessons learned. These communities could also reshape organizations by rethinking organizational designs, developing more formal socialization programs, and testing group configurations for effectiveness, and then doing the same for management and leadership practices. There would be much more in the way of movement across agencies and of interagency familiarization. Courses, fieldwork, tools, technologies, and decision aids could also move across agencies and communities of practice.

For some workshop participants, the implicit critique seemed too harsh. To be sure, there have been innovations in the way analysis is done. There is more use of phone-calling of colleagues, including abroad, and more conferences bringing in outsiders, and in the Directorate of Intelligence (DI), the Strategic Assessments Group is itself an innovation. Still, there are few professional methodologists in the intelligence community, and many innovations founder on the trade-off between efficiency and secrecy.

There were also questions about what the customers of intelligence want. In general, they are not interested in *how* an answer was reached; they are, in that sense, not much interested in methods either. They want an *answer,* preferably a single, on-point answer. Yet, that reduces intelligence to being "plumbers," a metaphor that runs through the literature, and sometimes consumers *are* interested in how intelligence reached its conclusions.

Thinking Tools

"Thinking tools" can help analysts move from deductive modes of thought to inductive ones. All humans are bounded in their rationality, and they operate on the basis of mental models. If the world is driven by a relatively clear "in-box," the answer is easy: Hire a good lawyer to process the material. But the world has changed, and it is easy for humans to be left floating. Moving from deduction to induction, or to some hybrid of the two, is no mean feat; it is moving to a "string of pearls." We are all too comfortable with point predictions. But predictions coming from astronomy and physics will not hold for the world we confront.

In this world, thinking with a "bare brain" is like doing carpentry without tools. We need tools for thinking, and lots of them. How to choose those tools is a key question, the answer to which can be arrived at by considering five dimensions of a problem:

- Type of problem – simple/complicated/complex/chaotic?

- Available information – quantity/type?

- Task – understand present/imagine future/risk analysis/options development/ reasoning?

- Group mode – lone ranger/hierarchical group/ad hoc/edge?

- Stage – divergent/convergent?

One strategy is to concentrate on tools that work across the "edges" of organizations – that is, allow people from different organizations to cooperate, and never mind what the formal organization charts indicate.

There are lots of autonomous actors, and the future is path-dependent, not simply random. To the extent that cognitive symbols guide behavior, those symbols are useful as clues to analysis. Thinking tools strive for a hybrid, agent-based analysis model guided by deductive axioms. Then, the analyst can run the model and get inductive results. It is important to bear in mind, though, that the model is just a model; it is not reality. As said earlier: the map is not the terrain. To believe otherwise is, to use another saying, like entering a restaurant where the patrons are eating the menus.

In this model, the connectors derive from a "story" line, but then can generate a collection of scenes or stories. The result is a "cognitive blending" of mental space and generic space. Why should this happen? New knowledge is different from new inputs to the model and allows the analyst to create something different. Otherwise, analysts, like other people, are inclined to shrink their mental space when they get too busy.

This process of cognitive blending can be demonstrated by the case of Ramsi Yousef and plans for his attack on the World Trade Center in 1993. Actors create a variety of strategies to achieve their goals. We cannot assume that they do not adjust or adapt to changing conditions. They examine all types of contingencies and they update their plans when they receive new information.

If we rely on simple deduction, or a top-down view, for trying to predict what an actor might do, we create a simple model for how the actor might behave that allows us to sort through relevant data, but we could leave out some crucial evidence or crucial features of a strategic situation. If we rely on induction, or a bottom-up view, we get a complete picture but have no way of organizing evidence to understanding the strategic incentives and constraints facing an actor.

The blending process is a combination of deduction and induction. Blending would examine Ramsi Yousef's broad goals and the options available to him to reach those goals, but would also look at the different networks or obstacles at ground level that might force him to change his strategy. Blending moves us from static to dynamic analysis. The analyst or expert first constructs some generic spaces as a starting point for this blending across "integration networks."

Break-Out Groups, II

The workgroups were asked to work from their individual perspectives but, again, to not be unduly constrained by them. For this session, the emphasis was less on a diagnosis than on a prescription: What might be done?

Cognition

Critical thinking will be key to analysts in the future who must learn to question their own assumptions about what they know. Now, analysts mostly operate from the seat of their pants. They can, however, be taught new techniques for escaping from the confines of some cognitive processes. Some of those techniques need to be automatic, given that intelligence now deals not with too little data, but with too much data. To be more effective, analysts need strategies for deciding how and when to arrange data. There will need to be a new emphasis on major learning processes. Currently, there is no incentive structure among analysts that encourages continual learning, such as developing new language skills.

Culture

The culture of organizations plainly matters as much as their broader cultural biases. For CIA analysts, in particular, only secrets – especially espionage and SIGINT – really count. There is reluctance among those analysts to venture too far beyond the latest evidence, and there is too much stove-piping. Thus, intelligence that was important to the tactical success of taking down the Cali and Medellín drug cartels failed to anticipate one indirect consequence – that traffickers would move their operations to Mexico instead.

In the current culture, it is hard to back away from making judgments, because if analysts do so, they risk losing their credibility. The bias toward making judgments, however, does not promote much learning. While there is more openness to external expertise than ever before, reaching out for that expertise is not really considered *intelligence*. It is also hard for intelligence to be as contrarian as it should be, because the senior "experts" stifle their juniors who might have "wild" ideas. Perhaps the rise of global networks – on issues ranging from law enforcement to SARS – will open up some minds.

Small-Group Processes

Plainly, assumptions are critical to analysis, both for individual analysts and, as those assumptions come to be commonly held yet often unrecognized, within a group. In current organizations, it is hard for analysts to "own" issues: Is that good or bad from the perspective of avoiding semiconscious assumptions? By the same token, models and thinking tools can be important in making assumptions and biases apparent. There are grounds for skepticism about such tools – especially about how user-friendly and transparent they will be – but it is critical to analysis to watch their developments.

The CIA at present is not organized to deal with cross-cutting transnational issues. It has tried to build some points of cross-cutting analysis, like the CTC, but it is still dominated by its regional and functional stovepipes, and working across them is difficult. Similarly, the CIA has fostered innovation in analytic methods, but in general has not accepted those innovations very broadly in common analytic practice.

On that score, the sharp reaction to this presentation on organizational cultures was interesting. It foreshadows the next workshop on organization.

Workshop III: Adapting Organizations

May 30, 2003

Headlines

- The challenge for organizations is not in decisionmaking but rather in "sensemaking" – not polishing a decision, but setting a direction for the next period of analysis. Sensemaking aloud –in public – can be especially valuable for intelligence organizations whose communications are private and written, not verbal.

- Strategic intelligence before 9/11 was good. Tactical intelligence was poor but always will be. Policy has to be framed without expectation of tactical warning.

- The intelligence community is still organized on an industrial model, not a knowledge model. Collaboration is more frequent at the top of organizations than at the working level, where analysts get rewarded for "writing your PDB item."

- The more venturesome Wall Street firms have "barbell" age distributions, teaming brave youngsters with experienced "gray heads." The more conservative firms, like the intelligence agencies, consist mostly of people at mid-career.

- The DI is hindered in exploiting information technology (IT) by process more than by technology – security rules, compartmentalization, budget cycles, and rules against individual analysts spending money or developing their own tools.

Framing the Task

This is the report of the third of four workshops part of a project jointly run by RAND Corporation and the Global Futures Partnership of the CIA's Sherman Kent Center for Analysis. The task of the project is to find useful frameworks to help analysts ask themselves, "How could I be wrong?" The group's working hypothesis is that so-called transnational issues, like terrorism, differ analytically from more classic state-to-state issues. Yet, transnational issues are important in and of themselves, and, thus, there is no need to exaggerate how they differ from other issues.

The first workshop focused on the issues themselves, asking– along dimensions relevant to analysis – how they differed from more traditional issues and how they varied among themselves. The second workshop concentrated on the individual analyst. It asked, what, from the analyst's perspective, are the obstacles to better analysis imposed by features of human cognition, by cultural biases, or by the effects of small group processes?

The central focus of this third workshop was organization and process more generally. Does the existing shape of intelligence organizations advance or impede analysis of transnational issues? If it's the latter, what should be changed? What could be changed? The topic of the workshop was not limited to information sharing, which is necessary but not sufficient. Nor was the topic the broader reorganization of the intelligence community. Rather, the key question is how to create "open-minded" organizations. There was, for instance, alternative analysis aplenty before Pearl Harbor, analysis that got the fact of the invasion right. But that work had no impact, including on the mainstream analytic community. For this session, our outside provocateurs were Karl Weick, University of Michigan, author of *Sensemaking in Organizations*; Elaine Kamarck, Kennedy School of Government, Harvard University; Daniel Byman, Georgetown University, staff member of Congressional 9-11 Inquiry; Tom Davenport, Director, Accenture Institute for Strategic Change, author of *Working Knowledge: How Organizations Manage What They Know*; Bruce Berkowitz, RAND Corporation and Hoover Institution; Roger Kubarych, Senior Economic Advisor, HVB Americas, Adjunct Fellow, Council on Foreign Relations; and Maj. General John R. Landry (US Army, Retired), National Intelligence Officer for Conventional Military Issues.

Organizing to Avoid "Accidents" but Creating Room for Creativity

Sensemaking in Organizations

Looking at high-stress, can't-afford-mistakes organizations – from trackers of the West Nile virus to forest fire fighters to cardiac-arrest teams to F-104 pilots – reveals a common tendency to fall back, in times of tension, on previous routines. For instance, the original U.S. F-104s based in Europe had ejection seats that threw pilots downward, and so they were trained to roll over if they got in trouble so that they would be ejected upward. Then, however, when newer models ejected pilots upward, pilots in trouble still fell back on their previous routine and rolled over, ejecting into the ground.

The same is true of firefighting team leaders in trouble. Rather than sizing up their problem, they fall back on actions they have done before. Indeed, a lot can be learned about how leaders will behave by looking at their *previous* jobs; each level of action can be predicted by looking down one level. Events produce a brutal audit of pre-existing procedures, into which individuals in groups are often thrown back.

Every organization is a product of how its members think and interact. Knowledge is not something possessed in individual heads; rather, it is something the organization does together. For instance, child abuse was not really diagnosed before the 1960s. To be sure, radiologists saw broken bones, in different stages of healing, in the 1940s and before. But those reports were confined to the radiologists; they did not become commonplace among pediatricians. The diagnoses were sadly quaint: "bruises easily" or "spontaneous brain bleeding."

That changed in Boulder, Colorado, in the 1960s when social workers were added to medical teams. That addition produced changes along several dimensions. First, it increased the range of the group's induction into the problem, because social workers knew what to look for. Information was distributed more widely. Second, it broke the "fallacy of centrality": pediatricians had assumed they were at the center of a problem, so if they didn't know of child abuse, it didn't exist. And, third, the social workers could do something about child abuse. By contrast, if pediatricians had diagnosed child abuse earlier, they couldn't have done much about it.

We tend to take for granted a performance bell curve under increasing stress. Up to a point, tension increases the performance of the organization, but beyond that point it diminishes performance. Yet, that curve holds only for complex tasks or for poorly performing organizations doing simple tasks. For good organizations engaged in simple tasks, the curve is more linear: more tension increases performance.

The challenge for organizations is not in decisionmaking but rather in sensemaking. Why is it necessary to decide on something? As a firefighting leader put it, if you make a decision, you own it and defend it. A *decision* is something you polish. Sensemaking is direction for the next period. STICC is the acronym for the process – situation, task, intent, concern, calibrate. Of these, the two "Cs" are critical. The first C asks what is it that we should watch and worry about; the second C opens talks with one another, because vocalizing concerns and suggesting directions is almost always liberating.

Yes, the biggest challenge is connecting the dots, but the dots change all the time. Researchers at MIT and elsewhere have demonstrated that if people move quickly to decisions, they remain stuck on those decisions. How to break that inertia? The answer might be "public sensemaking." A leader might say aloud what he or she sees as the facts of the case, then say aloud which diagnoses would fit those facts, and then open the floor to wider conversation.

Hindsight is often no help because it can distort the diagnosis. Once you start with a bad outcome, then it is easy to assume that the entire chain of events – from perception to analysis to action to outcome – was erroneous. In fact, each of these four stages can be good or bad in combination with others that are good or bad. After the fall of Singapore, Winston Churchill developed his own protocol: First, why didn't I know? Then, why wasn't I told? Why didn't I ask? And, finally and critically for intelligence dealing with policy, why didn't I tell what I knew?

Re-Engineering Government Organizations

Since at least the time of Max Weber and the Prussian state, bureaucracies have been the implementing force in all governments. The information age began to break that bureaucratic monopoly, because states became no longer the sole owners of power. Moreover, states found themselves trying to deliver more information but were not able to do so in the routinized ways that had sufficed earlier.

The "post-bureaucratic" state faces at least three organizational alternatives: (1) It can try to reinvent the bureaucratic state, retaining the basic form of that state but borrowing practices from the private sector, especially to enhance the productivity of service delivery. (2) It can try to become "government by network," especially in social policy. That tactic derives from the observation that while the delivery of service is fractionated into stovepipes, such as intelligence collection, the recipients of all those separate services tend to be the same people. So, integrating service delivery made sense, and in the process governments realized that they are ineffective at some services, so it also made sense to involve non-government organizations (NGOs) in, for instance, mental health services. (3) The third alternative is "government by market," in which the government doesn't "make" or regulate markets but instead creates markets where none existed. This concept has been a success with the "bottle bills" that provided an incentive to pick up litter, and it has also worked well with emissions-trading schemes. The problem is that while the concept is attractive, the design is tricky, as California found to its chagrin in trying to deregulate its energy market.

Internally, then, the challenge for government is to match its form to the problem it is seeking to address. For intelligence, that means asking how it should organize to have a better chance of connecting the dots. Moving toward the form of a network seems key. So long as U.S. intelligence was monitoring another bureaucracy, like the Soviet Union, its own bureaucratic form was acceptable. It is not now. At the same time, the state has not gone away, so the right form for intelligence will not be "silos" but rather a cross-hatching across geographical areas, across traditional issues and new ones, and across tacit or intuitive knowledge and technical knowledge.

Knowledge organizations let information flow freely, but for intelligence that runs into secrecy, which impedes the flow. More cross-training and jointness can be a partial answer to that barrier. This seems to be developing in the Department of Homeland Security, at least among the set of agencies involved in controlling borders. In some ways, modern organizations may be too reliant on technology, like email, for it simply takes face-to-face contact to build trust. It also takes face-to-face contact to produce a tolerance for mistakes. Some agencies have even experimented with "forgiveness cards." It is ironic that while the tenure system of the civil service ought to make officials more willing to take risks, it does not seem to have that effect.

Externally, intelligence will have to reach out to a variety of unfamiliar networks, like the news media, banking, and healthcare. It will take new legal protocols, like those that are developing in criminal justice, to be able to share information with those networks. It will also take training to make use of, say, credit card networks. The external reach of government will also involve government by market, as the government seeks to protect information infrastructure or chemical plants, for example, by creating incentives for private owners to provide that protection.

Assessing Organizational Performance Before September 11

For all the postmortems presented so far, the trail of intelligence failure on September 11 is pretty bare even in hindsight. There was no obvious single-point failure, and strategic warning – in the sense of understanding Al Qaeda and the likelihood of an attack – was good. Immediate tactical warning was bad, but it always will be, and trying too hard for that kind of warning could harm the capacity for strategic analysis. Thus, the policy challenge is to look for possible actions that do not depend on tactical warning.

The terrorism shops within the various intelligence agencies were tightly focused on Al Qaeda after the 1998 embassy bombings, but the larger intelligence community was not well organized to deal with a terrorist threat to the United States. A kind of no-man's land separated the CIA from FBI cases and transcripts, or the FBI from the NSA. As a result, there was less attention paid to Al Qaeda in the United States than to Al Qaeda abroad.

To be sure, turf battles were not absent. But they are less important than the fact that, for instance, the FBI was not really in the counterterrorism business before September 11. It had no intelligence cycle in the sense that other agencies think of it. Its information backbone was woefully weak; it was "where the 386s went to die." Decentralization meant there were 56 little FBIs, not one, and so the organization didn't know what it didn't know.

Other specific deficiencies were that the area analysts weren't always deeply engaged in the terrorist target, for they had other customers with other concerns. That was true even of a terrorist country like Yemen. Too little use was made of open sources, a critique the Jeremiah panel strongly made. Inside the Yemen government, it is difficult to investigate Islam, which can, however, be done outside government. A lot of terrorism analysis is both far from the mainstream and in areas, such as financial flows, in which intelligence had difficulty being afforded access to the relevant experts.

As an institutional strategy, being contrarian is stupid, because the risks are high, especially in terms of crying wolf. On the whole, increasing competition among analysts – as is now occurring in the Pentagon while it develops new analyses – is a good thing. But there can be too much of a good thing if competing analyses merely overwhelm policymakers or let them choose analyses to suit their predilections.

In general, the usual lesson of postmortems is that failure resulted for want of money and attention. After September 11, neither of them is in short supply. Beyond that, other lessons of the September 11 tragedy need to be treated with care. Too much can be made of networking; as the saying has it, a network could not have attacked Normandy. And it may not take a network to fight a network. If anything, the intelligence community, and the FBI in particular, are already too decentralized. Al Qaeda will be forced to move from whatever place America chooses to defend, so probably betting on favorites is a better strategy than being systematically contrarian.

In the ensuing workshop conversations, it was learned that cross-agency contacts seem to be better at the top than they are further down, where stovepipes dominate. In many ways, particularly with the current administration, it is the policymakers who are contrarian, because they come to Washington with an agenda and predispositions.

Moving people, including ourselves, away from commitments or preconceptions is hardest when those views are public, irrevocable, and volitional. Intelligence, though, is usually private and written, not oral and "public" like the policy world. Indeed, intelligence is dominated by the tyranny of prose, in contrast to the military that uses graphics widely, or even the State Department, which has begun to encourage "blogging" (posting of Web-based journals). That gap between intelligence and policy makes it hard to achieve and to communicate strategic warning. Perhaps a model like Britain's Joint Intelligence Committee (JIC), in which policy types and intelligence are mixed up, is preferable.

In any case, the bulk of what is shared, and perhaps can be shared, is technical knowledge, not tacit information. In case after case cited in the workshops, there was tacit information – in the form of concerns that could not quite be stated in the usual technical terms – that did not get shared. That was the case in the most recent Space Shuttle disaster, where worries among engineers much earlier during the flight did not get shared with senior managers. In the extensive Los Alamos fire of May 2000, the crew chief called headquarters in the middle of the night with a premonition of disaster. When asked, though, if the fire had gone out of control, his only answer was "not yet," and so more firefighters were not dispatched.

There are innovative models for sharing tacit information. The University of Iowa Department of Economics, for instance, assesses future elections by "buying" candidates in a futures market; alas, the process works much better when the money at stake is real. The CIA Strategic Assessments Group has begun experimenting with this technique. In the Human Genome Project, 5 percent of the money allocated was reserved for the unexpected. Franklin Roosevelt as president relied on checks and balances among his advisors by giving them overlapping and sometimes competing assignments.

Break-Out Groups, I

The three break-out groups reflected in a more or less open-ended way on the presentations of the first panel. The idea of voicing data, arguments, and hypotheses – "sensemaking in public" – found great support, especially because it runs so much against the written and private nature of intelligence. Moreover, many "lessons" that are learned privately turn out to be wrong. Too often, networks develop at the grassroots or working level, but the insights or lessons do not move up through bureaucratic hierarchy. More training across agencies and more cross-training of methods also seemed valuable, as did learning lessons not from failures, but rather from successes.

The intelligence community is still organized on an industrial model, not a knowledge model. There seems no to be management system to even allocate people; in reality, there are thousands of stovepipes. In that industrial system, analysts get rewarded for writing their PDB pieces; they have neither the time nor the incentive, for instance, to seriously help another analyst with a problem. The DI culture runs against that. And so CTC did not grow even after the 1998 embassy bombings; EUCOM in Molesworth had more people working on the issue. After 9/11, it was all too easy to return to old patterns of not sharing information.

Before 9/11, intelligence was not really focused on terrorism, and the government couldn't do much about it. In those circumstances, the DCI's general warnings of an impending Al Qaeda strike went unheeded. Even fairly cheap measures, like hardening airplane cockpit doors, were thought to be too expensive.

So far, while there has been a big improvement in available money and top-level attention, it has mostly produced a change in activity, but not yet in organizations, let alone organizational culture. How can intelligence produce "space" for adaptive organizations? It might mean giving analysts a fifth of their time to adapt to change. It might mean designing organizations to evolve over time and retiring legacy systems with the determination to "never to do that again." Or it might mean "mod squads" of young analysts with few preconceptions. Unfortunately, many of these innovations run into obstacles posed by security systems.

Looking to the future, the FBI is critical. It is, potentially, at the center of local networks of tacit knowledge – i.e., the buzz on the street. Yet, it was deeply affected by the investigations of the 1970s, and the tradecraft for domestic intelligence is different from that for law enforcement.

Models of Managing Information in Organizations

When PanAm was failing, the head of customer relations asked his team to randomly survey the company's 200 best customers. Even putting that list together was not easy; there were no phone numbers to go with the customers' names. The eventual phone survey results were damning, yet all that information about customers' bad experiences had never been collected, let alone analyzed.

Four overlapping models, mostly from the private sector, suggest ways of thinking about information management:

- *Information ecology.* The first models of managing information – on which businesses, and the Pentagon, spent a lot of money – were based on analogies with machine engineering. Information was like water, to be either dammed or channeled. These models omitted human factors and were colossal failures. From these failures, the "information ecology" model developed. It looked at three overlapping environments – informational, organizational, and external. The informational environment included factors like architecture, process, strategy, staff, and organizational culture and behavior, which were key but usually neglected by companies. A final factor was a typology for the "politics of information" –

monarchy, federalism, or feudalism. Not surprising, most companies had the last form of politics. The organizational environment included the nature of the business; physical locations – businesses scattered all over the globe will find it hard to share tacit information; and technology, which always gets more attention than it deserves. The business environment was composed of similar factors – business, information, and technology. The metaphor of ecology implies that there is a lot going on, but that purposive action can improve outcomes.

- *Knowledge management.* Here, the key insight is that what is to be managed is not information but knowledge. This model focuses on resources first – people, process, and technology. The key to process is making "amateurs" good at their tasks. For intelligence, the process would be producing papers. Yet metrics for judging the worth of knowledge management, such as return on investment (ROI), were hard to come by, and as a result, now that times are harder, firms are cutting back on these activities.

- *Turning data into knowledge.* These kinds of models are also called "business intelligence" or "executive support." They suffer from the fallacy that technology can solve information problems. Rather, technology and data are only the starting points. The challenge then is to adapt organizations and their culture so that decisions are actually made on the basis of data. With that in place, then other skills and experience are required – for instance, top-flight statisticians to guide data mining and people who can explain the results. Finally, it is crucial to have a strategy to guide the analysis, otherwise data warehouses become data landfills. It is easy for the transition from data mining to data analysis to become mysterious. Again, outcome measures are necessary – behavior, process and program, and financial measures.

- *Attention economy.* This is a new lens focused on information management, one that recognizes that what is in short supply is not information but the attention of senior leaders. That shortage has been driven by the vast increase in information, by how fast it changes, and by the leaning-down of organizations, which leaves fewer people to handle information. The key factors in this model are ways to measure attention; technology; physiology and biology – experiments show, for instance, that multi-tasking is impossible; and what it is that gets attention. The last factor has spawned studies on lessons learned from the "attention industry" – newspapers, advertising, and entertainment. Finally, the lessons are applied to the various business areas – strategy, education, leadership, and intelligence.

All these models deal mostly with what concerns U.S. companies – technical knowledge, not tacit knowledge. Moreover, there is as yet little experience on how well virtual sharing works. Videoconferencing seems richer than email, and it does seem obvious that if teams spend some "face time" together early on, virtual forms are more fruitful later. Can lost knowledge be recaptured in these models? Only very specific information or knowledge can be; the accumulated experience of, for instance, Los Alamos nuclear scientists who retire is hard to re-capture.

Perspectives on Information Sharing, Analysis, and Organization

Wall Street and the Private Sector

Here are ten lessons from the private sector:

- Markets are always wrong. There are three views about tomorrow. The two most common views are extrapolation and reversion (toward the mean), but markets can also level off and simply dawdle. Thus, at any given moment, two of the three views will be wrong.

- Wall Street takes the market price feedback seriously, a reminder of our fallibility. To hold onto a particular position for some doctrinaire reason is disastrous.

- Markets are moved by stories, not by data. At the beginning of 2003, 57 or 59 analysts surveyed in one assessment thought that interest rates would go up. That was the prevailing story, and it turned out to be stunningly wrong, as interest rates reached their lowest points in a generation. So it is always important to ask, what change in the story would change people's minds?

- To anthropomorphize markets is silly. They don't "think" anything. There has to be someone on the other side of any trade. On Wall Street, any positions taken are liquid and can be changed very fast. By contrast, when drug companies take a "position" on a drug, they make a very large, lumpy bet.

- Smart market people seek *disconfirming* evidence. They seek to overturn their priors. Postmortems are key, especially postmortems of successes.

- Data has been miniaturized. Technology now facilitates data gathering and turning out charts. At Kaufman in 1980, it took 40 analysts to do what can now be done with seven. Outsourcing empowers small operations.

- Knowing who knows what is crucial. On Wall Street, there is a host of people who know a given company – from stock sellers and buyers, to credit analysts, to raters and regulators, to former employees and competitors.

- Still, knowing the numbers is crucial. It is also impossible, and in that sense the whole school of rational expectations is a myth. Intelligence, though, does have the advantage of being able to get information that would be illegal to obtain in the private sector.

- Everyone except a market indexer is, by definition, contrarian. As the active traders become more numerous, market volatility will increase.

- People have a comparative advantage in some areas. Michael Jordan was a great basketball player but a mediocre baseball player. On the Street, stock pickers and market timers are very different. The former are detail oriented, like intelligence warners; the latter are more strategic. In that sense, larger firms can specialize to some benefit.

The implication of these lessons is that reward structures for analysts should be akin to the scoring of diving competitions. They should both ask how good a dive is and how difficult it is, not just simple scavenger hunting. Analysts should first ask, what do you think? But then there's also the George Shultz question: If you are wrong, how are you likely to be wrong? The first analysts who saw warning signs about Enron were those who noticed that it was not paying much taxes while reporting huge profits; it was lying either to the IRS or to the Street. Similarly, an early sign that WalMart meant to drive K-Mart out of business were signs in the former's stores offering to beat any K-Mart price.

Interestingly, the venturesome small firms on the Street have a "barbell" age distribution, teaming brave youngsters with experienced gray heads. The big companies tend, by contrast, to have more people in middle age. Are policymakers liquid or lumpy in their thinking? The conceit of intelligence is that it is the possessor of truth. By contrast, policymakers either come into office with a "story" or soon acquire one.

The Military

Terrorism is like war in that it uses violence for political ends, however incomprehensible those ends sometimes seem to be. Thus, it needs to have logistics, intelligence, and the like. War is designed to produce change, and so it creates the risk of dramatic failure or can produce breakthroughs. Nations are always trying to change the correlation of their forces, at least in the perception of their would-be foes, and so they seek allies. And they use denial and deception to exaggerate their power and break the will of their opponents. War by its nature involves deprivation, friction, and surprise. Misperception can arise from technical flaws in communications or sensors, from human factors such as preconceptions or fatigue, and from deliberate distortion.

How to cope with these distortions? Operationally, the principle of the offensive dictates some terms of engagement. Armies can also employ information operations and psyops. These all apply to terrorism, yet attacking terrorists is long-term and intrusive, not the sharp but short interventions that usually characterize war. In that sense, fighting terrorism is akin to battling insurgencies. Organizationally, armies are centralized to keep a unity of effort, because some battles matter more than others, and because information is not free. Commanders can delegate authority but not responsibility. The need to integrate intelligence, communication, and ISR leads to network-centric warfare.

Procedurally, militaries make campaign plans with lots of branch plans if something goes wrong. All these ideas apply to other organizations. If the consequences are large enough, then the military tries to take control of its operating environment. We are not yet at that point with terrorism, but if the threat became serious enough, we would take more control of the environment – at home as well as abroad. The intelligence community seems very distant from its customers, and it doesn't do enough lesson learning.

Information Technology in Intelligence

In looking at the DI's use of IT, the main issues were not those of technology but of practice. First, security rules limited technology and meant that analysts tended to see IT as a threat, not as an opportunity. The analysts were less creative and didn't drive the technology. Second, compartmentalization, especially between the DI and the DO, further slowed the pace of technology. Third, the annual procurement cycles on which the government lives are shorter than the cycle time for IT. Fourth, the ethos of coordination meant that bureaucratic processes set the pace for intelligence, not the cycle of IT. Finally, analysts can't spend money or develop tools on their own.

As a result, the DI cannot fill the bill of an "agile intelligence organization." It cannot move people around quickly if need be; it cannot draw easily on outsiders and their information; and it cannot exchange data freely.

As is now common wisdom, intelligence faces a very different threat environment after the Cold War and 9/11. The threats are many and diffuse, not few; discontinuous, not evolutionary; tactically rapid, not slow; and diffuse geographically, not concentrated. The Cold War intelligence challenge was akin to the intelligence challenge of Pearl Harbor, sorting out signals from noise against a defined target. During the Cold War, moreover, there were not a lot of signals to look for. Now, the challenge is to look at a sea of data and discern warning patterns by drawing on the data, on experience, on connections to other organizations, and perhaps on luck. For that reason, agile organizations are needed.

Before 9/11, there was no deep-cover HUMINT on the terrorists, and so there was little SIGINT. Perhaps as important, while there was strategic warning, that warning engendered little response. It was not like DEFCONs in the military that cause military organizations to take action. In intelligence, by contrast, there was, and is, no easy way to shift people or accounts in response to strategic warning.

What to do about this? In the short run, encouraging, not discouraging, analysts to have their own websites would let people new to an account quickly read into it. The real intellectual property of intelligence derives from the time analysts spend each day sorting through the new take of information. In that sense, the DI practice of separating managers from senior analysts, while it is understandable to protect senior analysts, is a bad idea. In the longer run, innovation does run into existing security practices, which need to change dramatically in the direction of risk management.

At present, the DI's age distribution is heavily in the middle-age range, like the more conservative big Wall Street firms. As it is now hiring rapidly, it will move toward a barbell distribution, and it should make special use of its younger cohorts' energy, creativity, and IT savvy. Should it separate the young people into special "mod squads" or, like the smaller Wall Street firms, team them with very experienced analysts?

Break-Out Groups, II

In brief sessions, the groups continued reflecting on the day's themes. In one group, there was considerable push-back on the critique of the DI. It seemed to be better than it was advertised to be. Making best use of the new hires would mean teaming them with older colleagues, not isolating them.

The barriers to collaboration arose again and again. Analysts don't know where to go for collaborative opportunities, and don't have an incentive to cooperate. It was argued that while principals often do cooperate, the worker bees do not. And security practices raise the barrier to collaboration even higher, although only a tenth or a twentieth of the information that CIA analysts use is really secret. There is no security theory and no tradition of risk management. By contrast, in war and in the military, people have to collaborate or else other people will die.

The barrier to cooperation becomes a barrier to learning lessons. In order to make their own mark in an agency, analysts may stop doing what had been effective. There is little institutional lesson learning and little motivation to make use of what has been done before.

Coda: Looking Again at 9/11

In looking over the shoulder of, first, the congressional investigators and, more recently, the national commission, the forensic trail of 9/11 becomes clearer. Al Qaeda, a "venture capital" organization, declared war on the United States in a *fatwah* in May 1996; that *fatwah* was quoted in the New York trials in 2001. There was a lot of information tied up in the courts and in trials. But the trail of Al Qaeda and its links to other organizations are emerging. They are not separate. Rather, they are affiliates to different degrees, but all share a common enemy.

The investigations go back to the first principles of how to do strategic intelligence. More contact with outsiders and more use of open sources are important. Organizations need to know what's known and what isn't known. Clues are just that, clues, and need to be followed up with more serious analysis. In that sense, DI leaders have reason to regret their decision to stop reviewing longer research papers because, as a result, those papers stopped being career enhancing and so are done less often. Much of what intelligence writes, it writes for itself. That is all the more true now, when deep strategic research remains to be done.

The clues were there. We had photos of an Al Qaeda meeting in Asia but then let two of those photographed in the meeting enter the United States. We know something of the network and its origins. People involved in the Africa bombings, some of them U.S. citizens, moved back and forth. After 1996 or so, all the data collection on Al Qaeda had to be aggressive, and that ran against the tenor of those times. Terrorism was treated as a law enforcement matter or, perhaps, as a damage-limitation exercise. Yet, while the terrorists are good, they are hardly the KGB.

Workshop IV: Communicating with Consumers

September 25, 2003

Headlines

- The audience is more important than the talk. For intelligence, the product is the analyst, not some written product.

- Alternative analysis for transnational issues is "structured sensemaking," which, ideally, would be continuous, creative, collaborative, and counter-intuitive.

- "Edge" organizations might be licensed around existing organizations to do alternative analyses. They would be small and flexible, and able to integrate data sources in a way that is difficult to do on a large scale given existing compartmentalization and controls.

- If the analyst is the product, then analysts need to move closer to, and interact more directly with, policy.

Framing the Task

This is the report of the fourth of four workshops part of a project jointly run by the RAND Corporation and the Global Futures Partnership of the CIA's Sherman Kent Center for Analysis. The task of the project is to find useful frameworks to help analysts ask themselves: "How could I be wrong?" The group's working hypothesis is that so-called transnational issues, like terrorism, are different, analytically, from more classic state-to-state issues. Yet, the transnational issues are important in and of themselves, and thus there is no need to exaggerate how they differ from other issues.

The first workshop focused on the issues themselves, asking how – along dimensions relevant to analysis – they differed from more traditional issues and how they varied among themselves. The second workshop concentrated on the individual analyst. What, from his or her perspective, are the obstacles to better analysis that are imposed by features of human cognition, cultural biases, or the effects of small-group processes? The third workshop assessed organizations. How are current organizations and processes within the intelligence community suited – or not suited – to the challenge of dealing with transnational issues.

The focus of this concluding workshop was dealing with – and communicating with – consumers, particularly questions about new consumers ranging from law enforcement, to foreigners, to the American public. What special challenges – and opportunities – are there in interactions with consumers over transnational issues? We were guided, for this session, by Rand Beers, former NSC Official; Robert Jervis, Columbia University; Thomas Schelling, University of Maryland; Michael Schrage, MIT Media Lab; Samuel Gardiner, National Defense University; and David Ensor, CNN.

What Has Changed and What Has Stayed the Same?

A View from Policymakers

For one senior policymaker, what was most striking over the decade and a half between 1988 and 2002 was the sheer volume of information crossing his desk. It was ten times greater now than it was before. Intelligence analysts are similarly besieged with information, and in that sense there is too much intelligence, and perhaps not of the right sort. What has stayed the same is that policymakers have no time to listen, or to read.

Knowing the customer was, and still is, crucial. Most policy officials at the assistant-secretary level and above have their own intelligence person. Like the PDB briefers, those people are good sources on what policymakers want. If a longer piece that a briefer brought were to get read, it was probably going to happen in the morning, and it depended on the briefer having a good enough oral presentation to intrigue the policymaker.

Something else that has not changed is the tension between current intelligence and intelligence over the longer-term. Policymakers are always biased toward the former, and that is precisely wrong. Without the context of an enduring story, dots are just dots, and remain unconnected. After all, the job of policymakers is to make policy, not to read intelligence. They need help with that task. In a sense, the relationship between an intelligence officer or briefer and a policy official is like that between a case officer and an agent. It is a personal relationship. It would also help to be able to give the policymaker some framework of intelligence products, and not just analysis – for instance, how does biographical intelligence differ from other intelligence? This seems to be especially the case for transnational issues and all the more so at the State Department, which still is dominated by the regional bureaus.

Seen from the vantage point of policy on transnational issues, what are the gaps in intelligence?

One is the gap in information on the evolution of Al Qaeda. It is still out there, so how it has evolved and will evolve is key. That said, perhaps the key is not Al Qaeda but rather the jihadist movement, of which Al Qaeda is only a part. As with the U.S. student movement in the 1970s, what is crucial is the larger phenomenon, and it is unwise to get too hung up on a particular organization, because the movement will replace its leader if those leaders are removed. We need to understand the organization and its recruitment patterns. A second gap is the drug trade, where our understanding is better than it is of Al Qaeda because intelligence has been at the task much longer. Still, our focus is very much on the Latin American region, and we don't understand the economics of trafficking in Afghanistan very well. We do talk directly to drug cultivators in Latin America, but that behavior is riskier in Afghanistan. A related gap in intelligence is in understanding synthetic drugs, like Ecstasy. We need to know of trafficking in those drugs early, and the first indications will come not from foreign spies, but rather from domestic emergency rooms. Intelligence has been work on organized crime for a long time. Given the profit from organized crime, it will not be eradicated, only managed. It will continue to move money, people, and death around the world.

A View over Time

Looking at consumers from the outside, one eminent scholar commented that the problem confronting the intelligence community is indeed a difficult one to solve. When he reads his students' exams, he can't help asking himself whether they were actually in the class. And he has power over those students in ways the intelligence community could only envy!

What's new in the world of consumers? His list overlapped with that of the policymakers. Policymakers are overloaded. When Dean Acheson was secretary of state, he walked to work, arriving about nine and leaving about six. He read books in the evening. It probably wasn't that he was so exceptional, it's just that the world has changed and so have the size and complexity of government. The vast increase in open sources is part of that change. The answers to critical mysteries, such as how Al Qaeda might evolve, can't be stolen; they need to be pieced together from a wide variety of information and analysis. A third change is the set of new customers, along with the rapid turnover in all customers and the fact that many of them have little experience with intelligence and what it can do. At the same time, policy these days seems to more and more often need intelligence to justify it publicly. This was striking in the case of Iraq but was true in many more cases as well.

While customers vary in their size and numbers, products remain pretty standardized. Customers may be adversaries – as well as being akin to case officers' agents – but, in any event, they see the world very differently than analysts see it. The advantage that analysts have is that policy officials *are* fascinated by current, secret tidbits, but that only increases the bias toward current intelligence.

Policy needs to understand what intelligence can and cannot do, and the responsibility for that understanding is probably intelligence's. If policymakers ask why they heard of a coup first from CNN, the answer is that it is CNN's job to get that news. It isn't intelligence's. Nor is intelligence's job that of a journalist, like Robert Kaplan. Policy officials need to understand that. The British Navy before the Battle of Jutland was misled when senior officers got the right answer to the wrong question. Then Director of Central Intelligence George Tenet did get President Clinton's attention, and he seems to have had mixed success with getting the attention of President Bush, so it *is* possible to get to customers.

It also remains the case that the academic study of intelligence is thin. Much of what exists in the literature is, understandably, historical, and the academy is turning away from military or intelligence history. What do we know from that history? First, policymakers bring to their jobs what they bring, warts and all. We know that customizing intelligence for them is crucial because they absorb information in different ways. It is easy to poke fun at President Reagan learning about his foreign counterparts through videos, but that was what worked. (And imagine when policymakers of tomorrow are composed of the twenty-somethings of today; their taste for reading as opposed to their taste for other media will be very different.)

For current policy officials, much of intelligence, such as the National Intelligence Estimates, is virtually unreadable. Professional editors would help. When Richard Neustadt wrote his postmortem on the *Skybolt* missile affair for President Kennedy, he knew that the writing had to be stunning or no one would have read it. Also from Neustadt, policy officials have to see that *your* intelligence helps them with *their* problem. The rub is that intelligence often creates problems, or simply overwhelms policy officials with uncertainty.

Psychological defenses also remain, which is all the more so if policy officials have strong preferences or predispositions. If they do, they will sop up confirming analyses and dismiss the rest. Before 1978, Iran was not a problem, and so intelligence could not give away its analyses. In those circumstances, perhaps the right approach is to pay more attention to those at the lower levels, the office directors and deputy assistant secretaries, to try to make the whole government smarter in the hope that the understanding will percolate upward. Getting policymakers to react to alternatives remains similarly hard, and so does red-teaming. No one wants to repeat the adversarial nature of the Team A/Team B analyses of the Soviet Union. Yet, these approaches, while time consuming, can generate unique insights. The challenge for intelligence is to fashion ways of interacting with consumers that yield comparable insights in less time and with less risk of producing hostile camps. Perhaps one approach would be to frame "if-then" propositions – *if* you think this, *then* the implication is that.

Some specific problems are also more difficult to deal with now. Yesterday's hard state intelligence targets seem easier to target than today's non-state terrorists. At least we know what those states looked like. Some generalizations were apt then. Now, intelligence has to be data-driven, but that creates possibilities for deception and results in that intelligence confronting a welter of poor information. Presidents could empathize with other heads of government, even hostile ones; they can't with terrorists.

This state of affairs suggests the both new tools are needed and perhaps new issues to study. For tools, the watchwords are *Darwinian, mutation, symbiosis, parasitic,* and *non-linear.* Perhaps there would be value in looking at the evolution of another "new" challenge – narcotics trafficking in the 1970s. How was that intelligence target understood? So, too, cases of both good and bad relations between policy and intelligence could be instructive.

Trying to Do Better with the Terrorist Threat

TTIC, the new Terrorist Threat Integration Center, was stood up in a hurry, tasked with producing a daily publication, the threat matrix, which is akin to the PDB. The TTIC did it, but it compelled policymakers to do the fusing of the information they received. In the process, three sets of issues emerged. Analytically, there is too much specialization of information and too little integration of it. This is particular true of domestic information. Moreover, the data are fragmented, and a lot of the data are bogus. There are few tools to "connect the dots," as was apparent, alas, in the summer of 2001. This situation suggests much more information-sharing is needed, a theme of all discussions such as this. But, technically, it is hard to talk across organizations. And, more important, all those organizations control their own information and security policy – i.e., "need to know" and "ORCON" rule. What is needed is more use of "tear-line" reports of sensitive but unclassified (SBU) information. There also is a need for a single authoritative terrorist database, and the FBI is tasked to create one. Unhappily, there are very many "Mohammeds" out there.

This is a period, though, like 1946-1947, when the definition of national security is being redefined. At some point, the National Security Act will be revised. For now, Congress feels ignored because TTIC is not part of the Department of Homeland Security. But there is a fair argument, given intelligence's needs, that putting TTIC under the DCI was a wise choice.

The ensuing conversations focused on roles. Policymakers read the newspaper because they or their bosses will have to react to the reports in it. So why not, in the words of computer whizzes, "turn a bug into a feature"? Intelligence could critique Tom Friedman or Robert Kaplan, recognizing explicitly that to some extent intelligence and the media are in the same business. Tailoring intelligence to particular consumers does tend toward current intelligence. In the past, everyone got the same "Model T"—what intelligence produced. Now, the community can't say no to any question, however tangential it may be. For some analysts whose main subject is now out of the limelight, like narcotics, the answer may be to connect themselves to priority concerns such as state failure.

Break-Out Groups, I

The three break-out groups reflected on the panel discussions, looking for factors that made consumers less or more receptive to information. Common threads ran through the groups, especially the observation that "ideological" or "committed" policymakers were almost impossible to reach, and so the right approach in those circumstances was to aim lower to work with less senior – and less political – consumers. For one group, that led to the search for how preconceptions might be challenged and for a "safe space" in which that might be done. The setting, including the physical setting, had to convey a sense of comfort to create that space. This group also thought that more open, unclassified material would open up the relationships. And it wanted more experiments, like TTIC.

The second group also focused on customers with preconceptions. In addition to suggesting that intelligence work with the permanent government, not political appointees, those in the group also mentioned hooking any analysis to what plainly is of concern to senior policymakers – the point being, again, about using government stability as a hook for the analysis of narcotics. The best time to get policymakers' attention is before there is ownership of issues or policies. That might be true now, for instance, of water shortages as a source of global conflict. The rub is that at this time, for that issue, no collective wisdom points toward action. And this group also noted several underserved sets of consumers – Congress, the press, and the public.

The third group found that policymakers' receptivity to analysis depended on analytic tradecraft, on the personal credibility of the analysts, on how well those analysts knew consumers, and how the policy process works. This group also saw policymakers in possession of ideological predispositions and filters. Other policy officials know they need help, but they also need to see, easily, that the analysis helps them with their problems. For all the change in the world, the NSC remains a pretty state-centric place, one that sees the world mostly organized by geography, and so it is on fairly stony ground for analysis of transnational issues. Identifying particular individuals – "gatekeepers" and others – who can be shortcuts to reaching policymakers is all the more key.

This group, as did the other two, looked lower in the chain of command in order to influence insiders to influence seniors. It also thought that creating an audit trail of what had changed in assessments of particular issues would increase institutional memory. Group members also favored continual exercises to learn lessons from recent analyses, despite the intelligence community's inclination to look forward, not back. There is no substitute for a good story and good graphics, but new paradigms and new products might help. Should there, for instance, be new products for particular individuals, or for new ideas specifically identified as such?

Reflecting on a Success

It has now been 58 years since a nuclear weapon was used in anger. Forty years ago, that long history of non-use wasn't imaginable, and 30 years ago C.P. Snow called the use of nuclear weapon a "mathematical certainty." The United States might have used nuclear weapons a number of times. When American GIs were encircled at Pusan in Korea, British Prime Minister Clement Atlee flew to Washington expressly to try to convince President Truman not to use atomic weapons. The success of the Inchon invasion made the issue moot. A more formidable challenger to nuclear non-use was John Foster Dulles and his attempt to remove the taboo from nuclear weapons, and President Eisenhower during the Quemoy crisis did talk of nuclear weapons as being no different from bullets. Were he and Dulles bluffing? Probably not, for nuclear artillery had been openly sent to Taiwan.

Yet a few years later, President Johnson talked of using nuclear weapons as a "political decision of the highest order." What had changed was not the technology – yields could now be made equivalent to non-nuclear warheads – but rather the perception of nuclear use. Peaceful nuclear explosions, enhanced radiation weapons, nuclear blasts for clean energy, all of these ideas died quickly because of the perception that they would lower the nuclear threshold. While the Soviet Union said publicly that any war in Europe would quickly become nuclear, it also spent vast treasures on a conventional force that belied those statements. Nor did Moscow use nuclear weapons to prevent its defeat in Afghanistan.

Israel's decision not to use nuclear weapons in a perfect situation for their use – when Egyptian troops crossed the Suez Canal in 1973 but were far from any civilians – suggests that the nuclear taboo may not be merely Christian or Western. India and Pakistan, for instance, have before them several models, both of which argue against using nuclear weapons. One is that it is taboo; using nuclear weapons would turn any state into a pariah. The other is the U.S.-Soviet tradition of non-use, lest the exchange get out of hand. What is key now is to get Iran and North Korea to agree to this line of thinking. For intelligence, that means careful attention must be paid to who gets nuclear weapons in new nuclear states – the military, intelligence, or the palace guard – and to what signs can be fathomed about what the regime thinks of nuclear weapons. To be sure, since even in retrospect we can't be sure what President Eisenhower thought of nuclear weapons, knowing what an Iranian mullah thinks will hardly be easy.

The non-proliferation regime has been, on the whole, a success. The United States could reinforce it by approving the Comprehensive Test Ban and by making clear it won't use nuclear weapons. Designing nuclear weapons for new circumstances is fine, but testing them may not be wise. It is a fair question whether terrorists and others can be deterred as the Soviet Union was. Certainly, for the United States to have taken down the Taliban regime was a signal and a deterrent. And Al Qaeda's threats to retaliate if the prisoners at Guantanamo Bay were mistreated suggests that the terrorist group does care about some things.

Perspectives on Communicating

Rhetoric of Persuasion

The audience is more important than the talk. Or to cite a Frenchman, le Play, "The most important product of the mine is the miner." For intelligence, the product is the analyst, not some written product. And so the key question is what kind of people the intelligence community wants analysts to be. There has been a lot of writing on the tensions, or personality differences, between analysts and policy types, but this group, like others, voted for a 20-percent increase in persuasiveness over a 1,000-percent increase in the use of information. The intelligence community doesn't have an information problem; it has a persuasion problem. For many people, it is better to let them change their own minds. Some will want to engage in arguments, while others will want to be left alone to cogitate on them.

Notice that innovators do not define innovation, customers do. This requires segmenting customers in terms of their time, their attention, and their accountability (who are their bosses?). The Big Lie is that they say they want better information and analysis. Wrong – in fact, what they want are predictions. But that is not possible. So, intelligence does need to redefine expectations. Here, the equation is

If the policymaker is at least as willing to change his or her mind as to cover a certain body part, that signifies intellectual integrity. If the equation is less than 1, there is little chance that will happen.

For the analyst, one mechanism might be explicitness about the level of confidence in the information and in the analyst's intuition. (The rub here is that for many interesting assessments, like that on Iraq, the debate begins where the information ends.) So, too, organizations are bad at producing an audit trail of how decisions were made. Intelligence might impose "may nots" – a one-page statement announcing that while differing interpretations were permissible, readers "may not" buy some particular interpretations or uses. Intelligence might be improved by the production of "advertels," 30-second video "ads" for particular reports. They would make the reports a lot crisper as well.

Another idea involves "Rapi-Sims," making use of the growing "spreadsheet-ification" of the world. These would be simulations on spreadsheets, not ones that take three days. They would let customers manipulate variables, and even data. They would be based on "just in time" manipulable models. These are all tools, not answers; they are intended to help policymakers create their own rhetoric of persuasion. So, too, the discipline of exploratory modeling, pioneered by RAND, lets analysts and policymakers "fly through" an enormous number of scenarios, looking for robust outcomes across variables, then display those alternatives graphically in ways that make identifying patterns much easier.

Gaming in the Public Sector

We know that adults retain only about a tenth of what they hear, so telling them things is an unproductive way to help them learn. So, the lesson of experience is to motivate people to learn, and not to talk to them, and gaming can be useful in this. Historically, war games were a form of practice when real war was not possible, but at the "high end," gaming becomes intuitive and almost Zen-like (recall George C. Scott as George Patton in the biographical movie saying that he "knew" Rommel from the sand table).

The experience of gaming with transnational issues has been mixed. On topics like migration across the Mediterranean, or drugs in the Baltic, or new Chernobyls, or piracy in the Pacific, it has been useful. It has worked less well, for instance, on hoof and mouth disease or for information operations when the information seemed to leave participants with only a fear of how bad the problem was or might become.

The military art moves from history, to theory or doctrine, to application. For transnational issues, there is little of either the first or second stage. The gaming required does not need to take three days, but it does require analysis. If the intelligence community conceived of its task as teaching adults, it would realize that it does too much in trying to talk to those adults.

A View from the Media

From the perspective of the media, especially the electronic media, communication is theater and drama. What is not said, or how something is said, can be more important than what is said. Policy officials may make news when they are trying not to, for instance by making a long pause before answering a hard question. David Kay, the weapons inspector now working for the CIA, was in town from Iraq the day of the fourth workshop to present an interim report. He had virtually nothing to report, but it was precisely that "nothing" that was the story.

Intelligence is the media's customer, and vice versa. The jobs of both are either the same, or the mirror image of each other. Media's customers are the public, but, then, in the final analysis, the public are intelligence's customers, too. Intelligence reaches them, and the Congress, primarily through the media. Is the media accountable for what it reports? No, but individual reporters are. They know that if they get it wrong, they will lose their access to sources. Their reputations are at stake. That doesn't mean they will shrink from taking a poke at the agencies on their beat if that is the story, but they will not do so without having their facts straight.

In other respects as well, the media and intelligence are kin. For the media, it is especially true that the analyst – in this case, the reporter – is more important than the news. For that reason, TV reporters wear makeup. They, too, face having to choose between short pieces and trying to draw viewers in for longer analyses. In either case, they need to tell a story. For them, too, fighting preconceptions is hard; try persuading today's producers that Kay's non-report is *not* news. Journalists also echoed an interesting theme of several of the meetings conducted for this study: Reading material aloud can be helpful not just in the presentation but also in communicating substance.

Is the public a consumer for intelligence? If so, intelligence has failed if 70 percent of Americans believe that Saddam Hussein was behind the September 11 attacks. In some ways, because the CIA is generally secretive, when it makes something public, it is assumed to be doing so for some purpose. It is assumed to be "spinning." Should intelligence then be more actively public in assessing mysteries, like Islamic terrorism, and if so, how can it get the public's attention by "sexing up" its work? Saying controversial things is all the harder, since dissent easily turns to appearing as disloyalty, especially in the eyes of committed executive branch policy officials.

Summing Up

Alternative to What?

This first of two presentations designed to draw the threads of the project together departed from the comment by Rob Johnston of the Institute for Defense Analyses: If the subject is "alternative analysis," alternative to what? Does existing analysis amount to much more than

"CNN plus secrets"? In fact, alternative analysis has a long tradition, and its tracks can be found before both Pearl Harbor and September 11. It was easier to employ alternative analysis for the former because the causes of Pearl Harbor were more bounded. David Snowden of IBM divides problems into four sets:

- Simple problems that are rule-based and have a solution.

- Complicated, multivariate problems, but ones that are still bounded and soluble.

- "System effect" problems that are difficult to reduce, and for which, moreover, your acts are crucial to the outcomes.

- Chaotic problems.

As analysts move from traditional puzzles to more complex issues, traditional analytic approaches yield their place to "sensemaking," something that is more intuitive. Mindfulness is critical, as it is with high-reliability organizations, which keep asking the question, "How could I be wrong?" Alternative analysis for transnational issues is "structured sensemaking." Ideally, it would be:

- Continuous.

- Creative – for instance, in constructing teams on the Wall Street model, bringing brash youngsters and seasoned veterans together, or mixes of personality types favoring closure and not favoring closure.

- Collaborative, with lots of lines crossing.

- Counter-intuitive, – searching for disconfirming evidence, not just confirming evidence.

Opportunities for face-to-face sensemaking, for thinking "out loud," need to be built into intelligence's IT systems. Intelligence needs to hire more methodologists and creativity consultants. Now, the DI culture is like that of a university, but it needs to become more like an aircraft carrier or other high-reliability organization. It needs to seek to avoid failure, not avoid error.

The Challenge of Alternative Analysis

The second summing-up looked back over the four clusters of topics:

What's different about transnational issues, analytically? They are less clearly shaped than traditional issues. They lack context or a "story," and they are much more diffuse. Information that is relevant to them is not in too-short supply; rather, there is too much information, but much of it is of low quality. And, in a sense, analysis of transnational issues is like some military analysis. It is a process of continuing updates, not organized around discrete choices. It can succeed or fail at any minute.

What's the challenge for individual analysts? Some biases arising from cognition or culture may be especially sharp for these issues. For instance, it is all too easy to stop any analysis by demonizing terrorists, because they are so different from us. Transnational issues impose the need for more methods and different teams to be involved in the analysis – requirements well laid out in the previous summary.

What are the implications for organizations? Here, the innovators seem to be "edge" organizations or small groupings, some of them virtual, that spring up around existing organizations. Paradoxically, place may matter very much in the sense that some of these groups, inside the security fence, go ahead and integrate very different sources of information, sources that would be difficult to get license – given the tyranny of ORCON – to integrate across the board. These edge organizations, perhaps a dozen people supported by another hundred, find "boutique" niches; they are not in the assembly line of analysis. And probably the people required for them are different – people who are very IT savvy and who know collection sources very well.

How to get the message across? Virtually all the techniques amount to getting closer to, and interacting more directly with, consumers, whether through new forms of product or through gaming or sensemaking out loud. All these techniques are based on the recognition that the analyst *is* intelligence's product. If there is an up side, it may be that the very shapelessness of these new issues means that the "story" is yet to be constructed. It can be. Notice how much the terrorism "story" has moved? At first, it was Al Qaeda atop subsidiary organizations; now, it is recognized that the network is much more fluid, and that some of the other organizations predate Al Qaeda.